Praise for *R*

I loved this book! Being with K_____
gift. Part spiritual director, part kitchen-table friend, Root gently
unzipped every article of anxious faith I own and left my "worry
time" self on the floor. Every chapter was a flood of relief. Don't
reach for this book. Receive it.
—Kenda Creasy Dean, Mary D. Synnott Professor of
Youth, Church, and Culture, Princeton Theological Seminary,
and author of *Innovating for Love: Joining God's Expedition Through
Christian Social Innovation* and *Almost Christian: What the Faith of
Our Teenagers Is Telling the American Church*

Receiving This Life is a blessing. Kara Root's honesty, relentless hope,
and fearless imagination empower me as a pastor to accompany
my community of faith courageously in uncertain times. Root is a
cheerleader, guide, and companion along the way of God. Through
stories, practices, and prayers, she shares her thoughtful exposition
on life lived in faithful rebellion against the way of fear. Her voice
is just what I need as a follower of Jesus in order to retune my heart
and rediscover my belonging in this noisy, busy world.
—Rev. Jessica Daum, senior pastor, First Lutheran Church,
Brookings, South Dakota

Reading *Receiving This Life* is like coming up for air. Kara Root's
words are a comfort to those of us who are still reconciling ourselves
to the lives we have rather than ones we want. She reminds us that it
is in the disillusionment of our own ability to be extraordinary that
we find God's gifts of grace and hope. The book reminds us that
extraordinary glory can be found in the everyday. In the knowledge
that we can only come as we actually are, Root shares her practical
guidance to draw us back to the God who is waiting for us to stop
and take notice.
—Becca Dean, senior lecturer in youth ministry,
Ridley Hall, University of Cambridge

Receiving This Life is a true gift of a book. Root is an inspired storyteller, and the wisdom and care shared in these pages will be life-giving and faith-shaping for pastors and lay readers alike. I will be quoting from this book and drawing from it as a resource for my own ministry for years and years to come. Again, what a gift.
—Austin Carty, author of *The Pastor's Bookshelf: Why Reading Matters for Ministry*

As a parent and a pastor, I'm constantly on the lookout for multi-sensory, intergenerational, interactive rhythms and postures that will ground and guide the imaginations and daily experiences of my children and my congregation in the way, truth, and life of Jesus. *Receiving This Life* checks all those boxes. The reflections, prayers, and practices provided by Kara Root are simple without being simplistic. Whether you are young or old, inexperienced or seasoned, you will be guided into a deepening awareness of the always-everywhere presence of God, and you will be inspired with practical ways in which to play your part in the "deeper, truer story" in which we are "saved by God acting through our smallness to achieve remarkable things." Because Root provides examples of "kid-friendly contemplative," grassroots-y ways in which we become fully alive human beings who bear the image of God in the likeness of Christ, this book has already become a go-to resource for me.
—Jonathan Janzen, pastoral elder, Highland Community Church, Abbotsford, British Columbia

In this excellent book, Kara Root weaves together deep theological insights with stories from everyday life. Real takeaways from the book are the prayers and spiritual practices that help the reader attune to God, searching for times and places where God is revealed to us in our lives. As a minister, I would gladly recommend this book for personal use, at congregation retreats, in Bible study groups, or as part of spiritual counseling. It is the kind of book you did not know you needed until you started reading it.
—Rev. Kjersti Gautestad Norheim, vicar, Church of Norway

From the moment I began reading, I knew I was going to love *Receiving This Life*. It didn't disappoint. Kara Root anchors the book in relatable moments. Full of wisdom, gentle reminders, and helpful practices, it calls us deeper into God and ourselves. Root reminds us over and over again that our chief identity is beloved children of God, belonging to God and one another. She calls us back to ourselves, helping us receive our lives as gift. Root has such an authentic voice, and she doesn't shy away from the ups and downs of life. This book takes us on a journey with her in such a resonant way, affirming it all and showing us a way through to the other side, where there is freedom, rest, and joy.

—Shannon Hopkins, cofounder of RootedGood

Receiving This Life

Receiving *This* Life

PRACTICING THE DEEPEST BELONGING

Kara K. Root

FORTRESS PRESS

Minneapolis

Library of Congress Control Number: 2023020143 (print)

Cover image: Colorful abstract art print cubism art style
©La Cassette Bleue | Getty Images
Cover design: Kristin Miller

Print ISBN: 978-1-5064-8890-5
eBook ISBN: 978-1-5064-8891-2

For Andy.
By your insatiable curiosity, dogged resistance to mindless living,
unwavering devotion to me and to our children,
persistent attentiveness to God's in-breaking,
and unyielding commitment to rituals, rest, and routines,
you hold me steady and gently remind me every day
to receive this life as a gift.
Thank you.

Contents

Part Four: Receiving What God Has Already Done

Part Five: Receiving What Will Be

Part Six: Receiving This Life

Introduction

The grace of God means something like: "Here is your life. You might never have been, but you are, because the party wouldn't have been complete without you. Here is the world. Beautiful and terrible things will happen. Don't be afraid. I am with you. Nothing can ever separate us. It's for you I created the universe. I love you."

There's only one catch. Like any other gift, the gift of grace can be yours only if you'll reach out and take it.

Maybe being able to reach out and take it is a gift too.

—Frederick Buechner, *Wishful Thinking: A Seeker's ABC*

The final week of my daughter's elementary school, the whole fifth grade went to a camp together. She had heard about this trip since kindergarten and was looking forward to every part of it, most especially the night walk with the science teacher, the slugs-and-snails class, stream studies, and the ropes course. The bus would pull away from the school at 6:50 a.m. on Monday, and she couldn't wait to be on it. All her stuff was packed and by the door, and the excitement was so great that it was hard for her to fall asleep the night before.

But in the middle of the night, Maisy awoke with terrible ear pain, which turned out to be a full-blown ear infection. When Monday morning came, there was no way she could go on the trip; she'd be seeing the doctor instead.

I drove to the school to let her teacher know and spent the next two days with a devastated daughter, feverish and heartbroken. But by the second night, the antibiotics had kicked in and she was almost back to 100 percent. I told her we would wake up early and I would drive her up to camp to finish the week with her class.

On Wednesday at 4:30 a.m. I gently shook her out of bed, and by 5:00 we were backing out of the driveway, preparing for our four-and-a-half-hour drive, which I would repeat in reverse after dropping her off.

Around 5:30 or so, Maisy, who up to this point could hardly keep the smile off her face and the wiggles out of her legs, got quiet and still. After a few minutes she said, "Mom, I feel *really* bad that you have to drive me all the way up there."

"You do?" I said. "Well, Maisy, I wonder if you can let that bad feeling turn into gratitude instead. Listen to me carefully: I am so excited to drive you up to camp. I know how much it means to you, and it makes me so happy to be able to do this for you."

Her eyebrows shot up, and she looked at me in wonder. "Really?" she asked.

"Really," I answered, unable to keep the tears from my eyes or the grin off my face. Her whole demeanor lit up, and gratefulness oozed from her until she was practically bursting.

"Mommy! Thank you so much!" she exclaimed.

I marveled at the sudden shift in her, from feeling bad that I was doing something for her to pure gratitude. The difference was dramatic.

These are both ways to greet a gift. One kept her (and me) captive to a system of judging, measuring, unworthiness, and transactions. The other set her free to receive not just the gift of a ride up to camp, but the whole rest of the week. Every moment ahead of her, this child was ready to absorb with delight—far more, I suspect, than she would have if she'd boarded the bus alongside everyone else. When she received the gift I was giving her in driving her to camp, she received her own life, all that was before her and within her, as an utter gift. The joy we both felt right in that moment could have powered the car.

Joy is the word we use to describe the energy of being fully alive, connected, awake. When we are fully at home in love, that feels like joy. Jesus said that the point of all his teaching is that we have his joy, that our joy may be complete. The inner life of Christ's own complete belonging to God and belonging to the world is joy, and we are drawn into that joy. Joy can't be produced or even pursued; it doesn't come from us. Joy comes to us when we are fully at home in love.

The crux of our faith as Christians is this mind-boggling story that the Almighty came into this world as a helpless baby, into the arms of those he came to save, to share this life with us, to be with us. And then Jesus died, taking all that separates us from God, all destruction and brokenness, even death itself, into God's very being.

Then Jesus rose from the dead. And the power of death and division was shattered by the unquenchable light and incarnate love of the world. And there is nothing, nothing, nothing that can separate us from the love of God in Christ Jesus. It's settled and final: we belong to God; we belong to each other. All of us. No matter what. Forever.

This is what Jesus trusted and embodied, what he died for and rose into, and what he referred to again and again as the kingdom of God. God is always bringing this reality ever more into fruition in the world. This is the final verdict over all creation, where it is all heading, and what unfolds along the way—our belonging to God and each other.

We get to share in that. We get to join in that. And yet . . . and yet we choose sin. Which is to say, we choose self-protection and division, isolation, destruction, and existential forgetting. Instead of abiding, we strive. Instead of resting, we strain. Instead of loving, we view one another with suspicion and competition. Instead of with gratitude, we greet the gift of our own lives with comparison and judgment. Instead of receiving our existence here with joy, we furrow our brows, and tense our hearts, and burrow into the cold comfort of worry, guilt, and fear.

But here is the free gift of salvation: our truest identity is that we belong to God and we belong to each other. That is our deepest belonging, and it cannot be lost, destroyed, or revoked. We are made in the image of the Divine. Loved by God completely and utterly, without stipulation or hesitation.

In this life, we will be injured. We will wound other people. We will experience fatigue, loss, sickness and suffering, loneliness and fear. We will die. These are inevitable aspects of being human for every single one of us, without exception. There is no escaping these things. And woven into the whole of it is God's redemption, always at work—despite, within, underneath, and through everything we experience. This life is infused with beauty and wonder, heart-stopping awe, and face-splitting, leg-kicking joy. There is no escaping these things either.

Our lives are a gift. Both the painful and the pleasurable are the ground on which we explore and experience our deepest belonging to God and all others, the place of practicing that belonging.

In this book I am inviting us to practice a kind of openness and receptivity to something we can't conjure or create. I am suggesting a divine presence is holding everything in love and longing to connect with us, and that an encounter—being touched by something from beyond—actually happens from time to time.

Sociologist Hartmut Rosa has focused much of his work on this experience, which he calls "resonance." He describes it as an uncontrollable occurrence that wakes us up, makes us aware and alive and present to the deeper *something*. When the world, God, a moment, something outside us speaks to us, and we respond—with awareness, gratitude, a reaching out toward connection, an expression of awe or gratitude—we are transformed, and the world alongside us is transformed in a way that is unpredictable and uncontrollable; it begins speaking to us. When this happens, we are experiencing resonance: we are touching joy.

Rabbi Simcha Bunim of P'shishka said, "Everyone should have two pockets, each containing a piece of paper. On one should be written, 'I am but dust and ashes,' and on the other, 'For me the whole universe was created.'"[1] From time to time, he said, we must reach into one pocket or the other. The secret of living comes from knowing when to reach into each.

I think most of the time we forget these messages are in our pockets. I know I do. Most of the time we are moving too fast, having more experiences than we have time to take in. We're disconnected and ungrounded, reacting, not receiving. Most of the time we skim the surface of our lives, forgetting to let life in. For many of us, for much of our lives, we don't notice that we are living. Most of the time, we forget.

I forget for all sorts of regularly recurring reasons. I forget because I, purposely and inadvertently, multitask. I try to transcend my own limits and capacities as one human being and accomplish more within each moment. This pursuit of productivity makes me less present and aware.

I forget because I feel afraid. I let worry and anxiety over what is and what might be speak louder than love and trust, and certainly louder than hope.

I forget because I compare, I hold grudges, I let the nudge of competition spur me into isolation and defensiveness and into the perceived need to prove myself.

....

1   Bunim is quoting Gen 18:27 and Babylonian Talmud Sanhedrin 37B.

I forget because I am in a hurry. I've swallowed the cultural lie that busyness equals fullness, and that life requires rushing and accumulating—if not things, then experiences—and then relentlessly, publicly demonstrating how well we are doing it all.

I forget because I am overwhelmed and persuaded by the loudness of the lies of our division, the bleakness of our collective brokenness, and dire impact of our destruction on each other and the earth.

I forget because death is terrifying and loss is excruciating. I prefer to avoid or numb pain, to use religious platitudes or psychological accoutrements to distract or soothe myself—or, more my style, to strive to control circumstances and mitigate risk—than to face the existential terror and randomness of suffering inherent in being human.

But thank God, I belong to a people who practice remembering together. In *The Deepest Belonging* I share some stories of Lake Nokomis Presbyterian Church (LNPC), the congregation I serve as pastor, and our seeking to live together in what we call the Way of God. This little congregation makes appearances here as well, as the source of many of the blessings and the setting for many of the prayers and practices in this book. We are being church together. That is, we are remembering God is real, seeking to be available to God, and practicing noticing God's presence and activity in the world and in our lives. We recall and rehearse our belonging to God and all others. We help one another recognize what we call the Way of Fear—when judgment, striving, competition, scarcity, and urgency make us feel that we are in life alone and against. And we help each other live in the Way of God—trusting that our unbreakable belonging to God in Christ, which stems from God's abundance and love, is inviting us always toward courage, honesty, and vulnerability.

Alongside this community, I have been slowly learning and practicing receiving this life. I am attempting to do one thing at a time and be present to the experience, what I've been calling *unitasking*. I have been learning Sabbath rest as a God-given antidote to fear and an invitation to return to trust. Through times of discernment and change, celebration and loss, recognition of milestones and meaningful moments in one another's lives, we're helping each other notice God and take up our calling as ministers all—that is, we practice the fundamental purpose of every human being, which is to care for each other as God cares for us. This means, with my congregation, I am learning the power and profundity of sharing suffering alongside each other and encountering Christ in our places of death and impossibility. We're inviting each other to the fullness that resists and opposes busyness. We're attuning ourselves to a further horizon and a deeper and sustaining hope at work in the world. And we're helping each other to engage the world's brokenness and beauty and to receive the gift of our lives.

When we forget, God reminds us that—not by anything we can do, but by God's love and act alone—we belong to the Almighty and every other human being in this beloved world being redeemed by God. We can't make it happen, but we can, as James Finley suggests, "assume an inner stance of least resistance"[2] to being overtaken by the Spirit of love, the moment of grace, the flash of joy.

Every human life is made up of brokenness and inescapable weakness, and also essential belonging and inherent sacredness. When we are persuaded to deny our deepest belonging to God and each other, a moment of resonance

2   James Finley, *Meister Eckhart's Living Wisdom: Indestructible Joy and the Path of Letting Go*, audio lectures (Sounds True, 2015).

returns us to our belongingness.[3] When we are determined to transcend our fragile limits and shared humanity and act as though we are invincible or alone, a brush with death in the form of humiliation or failure, a medical reminder of our mortality, or an experience of suffering or loss invites us to dip into one pocket: "I am but dust and ashes." And when we're imprisoned by our conflict and confines, and we lose sight of our glorious shared belovedness as image bearers of the divine, a surprise encounter with beauty, a sudden moment of shared laughter, or an opportunity to receive or give help moves us to reach into the other pocket: "For me the whole universe was created."

This book suggests we can reach more often into the pockets of remembering. We can exercise our availability and openness to being encountered. We can help each other seek the meaning inside experiences and let it shape us. We can practice belonging to God and each other, rehearse it, let it order our living. We can actively cultivate a stance of least resistance to being overtaken by a graced moment, a spark of connection, a flood of hope, a welling up of gratitude. Even in the terrible things, the painful things, the experiences we wouldn't choose and don't enjoy, we are held in the belongingness of God, which doesn't waver. God is present, and our deepest belonging holds us fast. Touching that reality feels like joy; we are alive.

Howard Thurman famously said, "Don't ask what the world needs. Ask what makes you come alive. Because

---

3   The Hebrew word *hesed*, which is most often translated as "lovingk-indness," is also rendered "steadfast love," "kindness," "mercy," "favor," "loyalty," "devotion," and "unchanging love." I argue in *The Deepest Belonging* that its meaning is captured best in something like "belong-ingness." See Kara K. Root, *The Deepest Belonging: A Story about Discovering Where God Meets Us* (Minneapolis: Fortress, 2021), especially chap. 3.

the world needs people who have come alive."[4] In a world of dire news, exhausting commentary, unrelenting evil, and a frenzied, breakneck pace, what radical and powerful antidote is a community of joy-filled and life-oozing people? What defiant and reorienting force is even a single person fully alive? Life is for living with joy. This is a book for remembering that. This book is a reminder that there is something deeper, slower, that can't be lost and can only be found. To attune our hearts again to God, to each other, and to our belonging to both is our calling.

To that end, this book offers five sections, five invitations of receptivity: receiving what *is*, receiving what's *difficult*, receiving what *God* is doing, receiving what God has *already* done, and receiving what *will be*. Each section contains reflections on ways we receive our life. You may choose to read the book straight through or to dip in and out here and there. These reflections generally build on each other but can also be read in any order.

Additionally, each section contains a chapter of prayers and a chapter of prayer practices. Prayer is a state of receptivity, an attunement to the Giver of life. We receive only because God gives. Prayer is being present and open to God, who is present and open to us. So, anything, everything, can be a moment of prayer. The prayers in this book—litanies, confessions, blessings, and prayers for specific circumstances—are simply specific ways to be present to the present God. They are meant to open lines of communication—to focus our attention and intention to receive from the One who gives.

The practices in this book are active and responsive ways of praying that engage the imagination and often the body. They include things such as journaling prompts,

---

4   Widely quoted, these words are attributed to Howard Thurman by Gil Bailie in *Violence Unveiled: Humanity at the Crossroads* (New York: Crossroad, 1995), xv.

walking prayers, ways to pray for other people, ways to pray for the world, and liturgies for specific occasions. To this end, the book may also be used as a resource book for prayers, prayer practices, and liturgies. I hope this is a volume you keep returning to—both for your own private devotional life and for shaping corporate worship and prayer experiences.[5]

Our living, every moment, is infused with the presence of God. God is at work all the time, everywhere, without exception. Ordinary experiences are brimming with meaning that we are not practiced at noticing or receiving. When we stop and notice, stop and honor, stop and receive the experience we are in—whether it is heart-lifting or heart-breaking—we reconnect to our humanity. We reawaken to God's presence. We open ourselves to the possibility of experiencing God right here and right now. We remember and rehearse our connection to each other, which can't be broken. We taste joy.

All that is before us, all that is within us, and all that is between us is an utter gift. The most fundamental calling of the human being is to receive with gratitude this life we have been given. This book is to help us practice our deepest belonging. Ultimately, I hope this book will speak God's grace to you in the voice of our heavenly parent in the driver's seat: "Here is your life. I am so excited to give it to you. I know how valuable this world is, and it makes me so happy to share all this with you."

INSTRUCTIONS FOR PRACTICES

All the prayer practices may be done individually or in groups. They can be used alone or combined in a service

---

5   All prayers and practices may be used in corporate worship settings with printed copyright attribution.

with multiple prayer stations. Adapt as needed for your context.

Journaling Prompts: With a journal, notebook, or paper, get comfortable and settle in. Give yourself time, perhaps fifteen to forty-five minutes. Turn off your phone and start with a minute or two of silence in God's presence. Then read the prompt and begin.

World Prayers: These prayers were initially designed for use with a ten-foot-by-ten-foot prayer map on the floor on which people could place candles or messages. People can gather around it and sit or lie on it. The world prayers here can be used with any size map, with an image of the world pulled up on a computer or tablet, and with or without candles. You may want to include visuals of other kinds as makes sense for the specific prayer experience or your context.

Walking Prayers: Walking prayers are designed for use in a labyrinth, walking in, pausing in the center, and walking out, but they can be used for an out-and-back walk or as a ten-minute loop with a predetermined halfway point. If you are doing this outside, you might use a timer to go in one direction for five minutes, stop and pause, then turn around and come back. Or pick a spot in your neighborhood that takes about five minutes to get to, go there, pause when you arrive, and turn around and come back.

Praying for Others: Most cathedrals have one or more stations with candles that can be lit to lift up in prayer specific people. While a few of these directions might prompt you to bring to mind certain people, most of the "praying for others" directions assume you come to the practice already holding particular people in your heart for whom you wish to pray. Lighting a candle is part of the practice for all of these, though not required.

Specific Liturgies: There are many specific liturgies and blessings in this book for everything from gardens to godparents, back-to-school to Bible giving, and letting go of cell phones to lighting Advent candles. Adapt as needed for your context.

In addition, many of the reflections contain in story form either intentional or accidental liturgies that emerged for particular situations, such as acknowledging dying, holding silence, bedtime rituals, and retreating. I would be so pleased and delighted to hear that this book helped inspire and empower people to come up with their own liturgies, for whatever situations arise in life, ways to intentionally be present to God and each other.

There are as many ways to practice the deepest belonging as there are people and communities living in it, and every new circumstance or situation offers new opportunities to practice and receive. May your joy and gratitude be awakened for all the ways you have attended to, and are right now sharing in, the work of God in your life, family, and community. And may your imagination be sparked for all the rich and beautiful opportunities to receive this life that you will discover along the way.

PART ONE

Receiving What Is

ONE

Belonging: Being Human

On a hot summer Saturday, I pulled into a line of cars among the fragrant pine forests of northern Minnesota to pick up my tired and happy child from a week of camp. He and his friends had had a wonderful time swimming, boating, singing, campfiring, Bible studying, and running around wild with credit at the canteen and nobody to tell them to brush their teeth.

The parents gathered with their dirt-smudged kids in camp T-shirts at the closing worship, and after some goofy camp songs, which the kids sang with gusto, the camp director stood up front to wrap up the week. "Hey, kids! Camp has been great, hasn't it? When you leave here, remember this: camp is a mountaintop experience, but what matters is what happens when you get home. You go home and be good. Make good choices. Be a good kid those other fifty-one weeks of the year. And then come back to us next year. OK?"

And maybe another time I wouldn't have noticed. But this time, for whatever reason, I heard what he said, really *heard* it. And I felt sick to my stomach.

Because kids at camp experience their belonging to God. In the gentle lapping of the water at sunset when the stillness and motion enter your soul and you feel the deep quiet inside where God sometimes speaks, and the creativity of a hut filled with craft supplies and another hour of free time stretching out in front of you to listen to what your soul wants to say with paint and popsicle sticks. In the encouragement and space to ask hard questions, and the chance to pray with people who aren't your parents.

They sense their belonging to all others. In the satisfaction of singing together at the top of your lungs, in the silly inside jokes that develop as friendships blossom, and the unrestrained joy of running and kicking a ball to someone with nowhere else to be but here, and in the freedom and safety and encouragement to simply be a kid.

At camp kids are reminded who and whose they are. It's not hard to pronounce a blessing on them, to point them homeward in that awareness. But this *is* hard for humans. It's almost impossible. We're nothing if not good at resisting grace and trying to find a way to earn what is a gift.

So instead of lifting up the gift of their deepest belonging and sending them home in gratitude, we'll put a heavy burden on kids, lock an unyielding yoke on their necks. *Be good. Make good choices. Make God and your parents proud.* We will echo the voices they will hear all around them the rest of the year, at school, in clubs, on TV. *Be a good kid.* We'll invite them into the weary existence of striving and comparing that we labor under ourselves. I don't blame the director too much. He was trying to say something helpful, perhaps even something parents expect him to say. And thankfully, hopefully, with the fatigue and excitement of reuniting with families, not many of the kids were paying attention anyway.

But this is what we do. We take the gift of God's love and acceptance and turn it into a commodity to be pursued and attained, held over one another and withheld from ourselves. Instead of receiving our lives, we strive to earn them. We begin young, figuring out how the system works and how to work it to our advantage. So much so that when wisdom personified, grace made flesh, love incarnate walks among us and invites us into life, we point out what he's doing wrong and refuse to listen.

Jesus says as much in Matthew 11:16–30, when he asks, "To what will I compare this generation?" (v. 16). And then he says in verses 17–19, in essence, *You are like kids who've stopped doing what you love for the joy of it, and now you play baseball with one eye over your shoulder to see whether your parents are pleased or disappointed. You play an instrument only for the applause. And you decide whether the picture you've drawn is good not by how you felt as you watched it appear in all its color and brilliance on the paper, but by the response the grown-ups give you when you hold it out anxiously before them.*

In fact, you're even more jaded than that. You are like the kids who get frustrated that you can't get other people to react like you want them to—and you're so caught up with manipulating a response from others with your music and your tears that you've forgotten what it was like to laugh in abandon, and to lose yourself spinning to a melody, and to weep openly with honest sadness; you've forgotten what it was like to simply be children. You don't remember how to receive, and you're too afraid to be real.

Then, like an exasperated mother, Jesus heaves a dramatic sigh, raises his face to the heavens, and intones one of those mid-argument prayers meant to be overheard. "I thank you, Father, Lord of heaven and earth, because you have hidden these things from the wise and the intelligent and have revealed them to infants" (v. 25).

So what is it that infants get that the brilliant and learned can't seem to grasp? It's not cognitive knowledge, and it isn't self-awareness, or grown-up self-consciousness. Power and might are the last thing infants possess, and it's certainly not the ability to make great choices all the time and never let people down. Infants have no résumés and no capital to spend; they can't take the entrance exam, schmooze the meet and greet, complete the assignment on time, or impress a single soul with their vast abilities or significant deeds.

To be an infant is to be helplessly and simply *you* and so to simply and already belong. Infants are children of their parents. Their identity is from the one who gave them life. They're dependent on their source. Infants belong not because of what they do or how well they do it. They belong, they are known and loved and cared for, just because they *are*.

So free are babies to simply be themselves that when they are sad, they cry. When they are happy, they laugh. And it wouldn't occur to them to imagine you feel anything for them other than unconditional delight and devotion. A baby wholeheartedly lives. Their only work is to learn to *be*. Their only job is to belong. To belong to their source of life and to the other humans around them. *My needs will be met. I can rest when I am tired. I can eat when I am hungry. I can sleep without fear. I belong to these people. I am held.*

Jesus's words become tender when he directs them back at the people he just railed at with this invitation: "Come to me, all you that are weary and are carrying heavy burdens, and I will give you rest. Take my yoke and learn from me; for I am gentle and humble in heart, and you will find rest for your souls. For my yoke is easy and my burden is light" (vv. 28–30).

Jesus is inviting us to take on his way of existing in the world. In the love between the Father and the Son, the love between a mother and her infant, we can set down our striving and be honest about ourselves and our need, and we will find rest for our souls. We can live in our fundamental, unshakable belonging as beloved children of God.

Jesus isn't offering a strategy to overcome our humanity, to fix the world how we think it should be fixed, to increase our productivity, optimize our efficiency, or secure our own safety. He isn't telling us to be good and try hard. He is inviting us to tell the truth with our lives, to live how we were made to live—attached to our source of life and connected to those around us. He's inviting us to be human. Our starting place, our primary belonging, our rest, is given, and in fact commanded, by the Creator of all, who rests.

The Bible often uses "entering the rest of God" as a synonym for God's salvation.[1] In other words, rest is how it feels to be saved from whatever keeps us captive, released from whatever consumes us, freed from whatever enslaves us, restored from whatever disconnects us from God, and delivered from whatever divides us from each other. Salvation is coming into God's rest. Being saved feels like rest, and resting is trusting in our salvation.

When the Covid-19 pandemic lockdown was beginning to ease, and life was shifting out of the sudden temporary global Sabbath back into busyness, my pastor group was meeting one afternoon in lawn chairs, sitting six feet away from each other in a park. My friend Peter said, "I've been thinking about 'sustainability' a lot this week. Why do we always act like 'sustainable' is a positive thing? There are a lot of things that are sustainable that are not good. Racism, clearly, is sustainable. We've sustained it for a long time." Then he asked, "Instead of asking if things are sustainable, why aren't we asking if they're 'life-giving'? The broken systems that perpetuate injustice in this country are sustainable, but they sure are not life-giving. And a frenzied, way too busy pace of life that drains my soul? I sustained that just fine. But it sure wasn't life-giving."

Modernity gives us stability and safety like no other time in human history could provide, but at the expense of our souls. In the constant human quest for *What is a good life and how do we live it?* our definitions have shifted. We mistakenly assume *good* means sustaining growth, maximizing potential, optimizing time, and extending

---

1   For example, Ps 95:11; Deut 12:11; Isa 11:10; 28:12; Heb 3:11; 4:3, 5.

reach, and *living* means achieving—and then working constantly to maintain—upward mobility (or at least steady improvement). We easily lose sight of our underlying belonging and our cosmic purpose, and we shrink down within the walls of our collectively confined minds and hearts. Amid all the pressure and momentum, we grasp the tiny reprieves and little escapes that keep our weary, isolated lives sustainable.

Eugene Peterson's paraphrase of Jesus's words says, "Come to me . . . and you'll recover your life. . . . Learn the unforced rhythms of grace. . . . Keep company with me and you'll learn to live freely and lightly" (*The Message*). We are saved not because of what we do but because of what God has done in Jesus. When we trade our yoke of nonstop striving for Jesus's yoke of rest, we receive our lives as a gift. We carry what Jesus carries into the world instead—absolute trust in our complete belonging to God and each other. *We* aim for sustainable. God offers us life-giving.

When my family was preparing to travel to France a few years ago, I listened to some French-language audio lessons to try to catch up to my kids, who had spent a week at French immersion camp. The lessons were unlike any language class I've ever taken. Instead of asking us to memorize vocabulary and conjugate verbs, the instructor jumped right into whole sentences and asked us to trust him. To show up and experience it, without trying to master it or get it right. Learning, he insisted, happens through forgetting and remembering. You don't memorize the backstory of your favorite characters on your favorite shows; you forget and you're reminded again, and gradually it sinks in and you know it. Learning is forgetting and remembering, over and over until it's just there, part of you. "But how can I remind you," his voice gently asked, "if you haven't forgotten?"

The unforced rhythms of grace are learned through forgetting and remembering. I forget and take back on the yoke of fear. I let myself get caught up in the frantic struggle to make my life count, to make my time count. I start striving, comparing, mimicking the divisive rhetoric around me, living in scarcity and urgency. I put that burden on those around me. And then something awakens me or reminds me—a moment of sudden, deep eye contact with my child, a shared laugh with a stranger in the grocery line, the smell of the earth after it rains—and suddenly I remember.

And that is how this life will go: over and over, I'll keep on forgetting and keep on being reminded, until grace becomes part of me. I with God, and Jesus with me, making my home in love. We humans will forget and remember, again and again, and we will remind each other. The deepest belonging is learned when we show up and experience it, without trying to master it or get it right. God sustains us in the unforced rhythms of grace.

And in our forgetting and being reminded, we might find ourselves trusting, even in difficulty, that our needs will be met. We might let ourselves admit we are weary and sleep when we are tired. Perhaps we will eat when we are hungry and cry when we are sad. We might lay our heads down at night and close our eyes without fear, because no matter what and always, we belong to God. From time to time, we even might sense our heavenly parent's utter delight in us, simply for being ourselves. We will be quicker to recall that we are held by someone stronger than we are and become more aware that we belong to all these people, and they all belong to us. When we surrender to the dance of forgetting and remembering, forgetting and reminding, we might find ourselves learning to live freely and lightly, and we will find rest for our souls.

When all is said and done, when we were gathered with our sweaty kids under the awning next to their piled-up luggage on that last day of summer camp, what I wish had been said to those tired, happy children is this:

> Hey, kids! Camp has been great, hasn't it? We've had such a good time here with God and each other, playing in God's creation! As you go home, I want you to remember that Jesus is with you always, here at camp, at home, at school, everywhere. You belong to God, who sees you at your best and at your worst and loves you, no matter what. This week we've been reminded that in our darkest, hardest, loneliest, and most lost places, God finds us, claims us, and calls us God's own beloved children. We got to practice together trusting that we belong to God and to everyone else. The other fifty-one weeks of the year, you might forget. You might forget your own belonging or treat others like they don't belong. We all forget. But God will keep loving you, and reminding you, and helping you love others. Come back next year, and we will help each other practice trusting God again, OK?

TWO

Abiding: Being With

On day two of my second-ever weeklong silent retreat, I was in the jittery withdrawal stage of detoxing from daily life's rigid attention to time management and measured productivity, and also from talking. Restlessly, listlessly, I browsed the monastery library. I casually opened a book about Sabbath, a dusty midcentury volume with outdated language and sketchy theology. I skimmed along, detached and a little judgy, and read about how God rests, so we rest because we're made in God's image. *We all know that.* But then I stumbled upon a sentence that said something like, "God rests because keeping this world going is not the only thing to God. God has other interests and hobbies; it's not all about us." And it struck me as so funny, so delightful, unexpected, and surprising. *We* rest because keeping the world going is not the only thing that makes us *us.* There is more to *us* than the work we do to keep everything afloat. *Why not God?*

Now, before I continue the story, it's important to acknowledge that this is a dumb argument. It makes God in our image. And referring to "interests and hobbies" when talking about the Fathomless Mystery beyond Which Nothing Greater Can Be Conceived is ridiculous and possibly borderline offensive. And, of course, there is no encountering God beyond what God does. We can only know the God of Israel who created the universe and comes into it embodied in Christ Jesus, by the act and word through which God reveals Godself.

But, something about the absurdity of the statement "God has other interests; it's not all about us" catapulted me back to the mystery. Had I inadvertently instrumentalized my relationship with God so much that I was like a child shocked to be told her mommy had friends *she* didn't know, or thoughts not related directly to the feeding and bathing and arranging of *her* playdates? Beyond the tending of human needs and responding to human demands, who is God? I felt a sudden, insistent desire to seek God without any agenda or petitions. What might it be like to hang out with God in the rest of God and not just the work? To seek the being of God and not just the doing?

I closed the book and returned to my room. Grabbing my jacket, I made my way through the silent halls and out the front door to the trails that wove through forests and fields. When I got to where I knew nobody else could overhear me, I let the curiosity and wonder rise up in me. On a quiet path deep in the woods, I cleared my throat and said, aloud, "Hi."

And at first I felt only silence—heavy, almost fearsome silence. As I walked along feeling emptied, open, willing to be encountered by this One I did not know (how dare I presume to know?), I grew conscious of the ground beneath my feet, teeming with life smaller than the human eye can see, and the wind against my face, moving the treetops above me and beyond them pushing clouds across the vast sky. I felt the silence in me reaching out to the silence beyond. I said it again, "Hi."

And then, *Hi* became a kind of centering prayer, both a reach for the unknown and a reoccurring invitation back to the concrete moment, to be available to be met by the mystery. And each time I said "Hi" I got a little thrill of awe. God was here. *God* was here. And I was here. I was *here* with *God*. We were hanging out. No other agenda than that. "Hi, God." "Hi, God. It's me." "Hi, God. Who are you?" "Hi. Thank you."

For the next hour, I hung out with God. Without any more clarity *about* God, I had a deeper sense of simply *being with* God. And how else do we get to know someone except by being with them?

"Abide in my love," Jesus says in John 15:9. *Abide* is not a word we use much today. I confess, at first, what I hear is, "The dude abides." In *The Big Lebowski*, Jeff "The Dude" Lebowski, an avid bowler and adept slacker living in Los Angeles, played by Jeff Bridges, abides. He says so himself 160 times in the movie. What he means is, "The dude lives in his unperturbable state of dudeness." He simply is. He abides. There is no striving in abiding; nobody says, "I was abiding so hard." It's a relaxing into, hanging out, lingering kind of word. So abiding in Christ is just being. Like the dude.

I regularly spend time at a Catholic retreat center near our home. When you book your retreat there, they send you a welcome video orienting you to your hermitage, and one of the things they say in this video is how people often ask what they should do. You're not there to *do* anything, the man on the screen assures you—you are just there to be. Calling the retreatant back to their humanity, he says, If you're tired, sleep. If you're hungry, eat. If you want to walk, walk. If you want to sit in the chair and rock and watch nature out the window, do that. You aren't here to accomplish anything, he says; you're here to abide in the love of God.

But the video goes on to say something interesting. Once we finally settle into accepting we don't need to do anything, we often turn that doing energy onto God. *I'll just be, God, but you need to do something for me. Give me an answer, some insight, a mystical experience, a message.* But that's not what this time is for either, the video says. You are here just to be with God, who is being here with you.

Abide. Linger. Be. Be connected. Be alive. Be here with God because God is lingering here to be with you. In Scripture, this word *abide* is actually not used for humans nearly as often as it is used for God. God abides. This is God's word first: God loiters with us. God hangs out with us in and through it all. We abide in Christ because God abides with us. We abide in Christ's abiding in God, because we belong in Christ's belonging to God. Abiding takes faith. We must trust that all our forms of self-preservation, isolation, and sinfulness have been overcome. When we let down our guard and confess our inability to reach God, there the living God encounters us.

Abiding is not a solo gig. It is impossible to abide alone in Christ. Abiding brings us back not just to our belonging to God, but to our belonging to each other. "God is love," 1 John 4:16 says, "and those who abide in love abide in God, and God abides in them." Abiding *in God* means love. Loving, being loved, love. And that requires other people.

There is no individual discipleship, no personal, isolated relationship with God. I do not experience Christ somehow apart from my life lived alongside, with, and for others, because Christ *is* God-with-us. That's not to say that solitude isn't essential, or that we can't get away, like I do at the retreat center, to hang out with God. But any connection I have to God *there* is inextricably woven into the connections I have with other people *here*. I am not me without them. I bring with me the joy and pain of those I love, and the sorrow of our nation and world. And I return from *alone* to *together*, to *with* and *for*, to *alongside* and *in*—with my family, friends, and community, to the whole world of which I am a part.

It is in and alongside each other that we find Christ. "God becomes incarnate so that man [*sic*] might contemplate God's face in every face. . . . Every face is an icon of Christ discovered by a prayerful person."[2] When we abide in Christ, we find ourselves living our unique personhood alongside the unique personhood of others, alive and connected, contributing to life and connection for others. We'll receive others, linger in life's pleasure, and share life's pain with others, standing by others and finding them doing that for us. God's love is embodied in us, between us; God uses our voices, and our arms and our eyes and our hearts, to love. And when we are loving one another, we are abiding in Christ.

When my son, Owen, was born, I was full-on in a blossoming love affair with liturgy, so I was determined to set up a liturgical bedtime routine for our new baby. I had a hymn to sing ("Evening Hymn") and a prayer to recite (by Dietrich Bonhoeffer). I printed them out to read each night until I could memorize them, imagining my child memorizing them too, and eventually the two of us reciting them together every night before bed his whole childhood. Night after night those first few months I held my tiny infant close to my chest and sang this hymn, whispered this prayer. The paper on which they were printed got soft and crinkled from being dropped under the rocking chair again and again as I worked to make this become our routine.

But something else happened instead. A song I made up became more prominent. It came spontaneously one day and became what I hummed when I'd rock him to sleep for a nap or when I picked him up because he was crying. The only words were, "Owen Andrew, Mama loves you." It didn't have any of the theological depth I had specifically chosen in the bedtime hymn. It had the inner logic of our relationship. What was conveyed went far beyond the words to express something real between us. And as we

---

2   Paul Evdokimov, *The Struggle with God* (Mahwah, NJ: Paulist Press, 1966), 178.

---

were present to each other in the moment, gradually the hymn fell away, and the Bonhoeffer prayer disappeared, and bedtime developed its own ritual of rocking and singing and prayer, and an inexplicable request I made once and never stopped making, night after night for eighteen years, for "sweet and wonderful dreams." The liturgy I had superimposed in the beginning made space for a liturgy of connectedness to evolve from within.

For my daughter, an unexpected bedtime routine emerged for a few years. Maisy struggled with anxiety when she was young, and one strategy we discovered was to save up her worries for the end of the day and set aside a time to let them all out. So when she started fixating on something she was worried about, I would say, "Maisy, save that for Worry Time."

And she would ask me as she got ready for bed, "Mommy, can we have Worry Time tonight?"

Then Worry Time would begin, and she would empty out every worry she had held onto in the day, and I would hold space for more as they came up, until she felt finished with them all, and we'd give them to God and ask God to hold them.

I didn't realize how much this meant to her until one evening in our prayer service at church, when we wrote gratitudes on paper hearts and placed them on a floor map of the world. Maisy, in her second-grade penmanship and spelling, wrote that she was thankful that "Me and my mom hav worry time gust to get away the worrys."

Somehow, in making space for what was in her to come out, we found ourselves reconnected to God and each other, and she could reclaim her humanity as one who is held securely in that belonging, in the love more powerful than death, more enduring than any of the things she worried about. And I hadn't realized it was so powerful until she expressed her thankfulness for this pocket of time we had together each night.

There is a way of being human—being with, for, along-side—that brings us back to our humanity. It's a choice to be present and open to the other. To step out of urgency and agenda and simply be. To be clear, many, many bed-times in my kids' childhood, this did not happen. I wanted to be finished parenting and I wanted tired children to go to sleep, so it was perfunctory and succinct. But other times, I found myself surrendering to love and leaning on the cord that binds us to each other, being present, being with. Just being. No agenda, open to one another. In those moments, I was abiding not only with my children but also with God. We together were abiding in Christ, who met us within our abiding with each other.

How do we feel God's love? In the love of others. How do we feel God's love? When we love each other. It's not an abstract, spiritual, distant thing. It is a concrete, real, tangible thing. When we love each other, see each other, hear each other, are present to each other, God lives in us, and God's love is completed in us. When we receive one another, we receive Christ.

But lest we slip back into thinking that "being loving" is a task to achieve, that right after we're finished scrubbing the sink and taking out the garbage we need to make our-selves into loving people, we come back to the abiding, the being loved already and completely by a loving, loitering God. It's not even our love, after all; it's Christ's love we are abiding in. We're recipients and conduits—like branches on a vine—just sharing it, breathing it, and passing it around. We are just learning to hang out in the love of God that sustains us all.

THREE

Availability: Being Here

I grew up in a pretty messy home. I am not sure how it compared to other homes, though I wondered about this a lot and felt a sneaking suspicion we were outstandingly untidy, like maybe worse than everyone I knew. When you came over to our house for dinner, what you didn't know was that several grueling hours of family scrambling went into getting things ready for you. Cleaning (which often meant stuffing things into drawers and cupboards where they couldn't be seen) was frenzied and fraught, so that by the time you were casually welcomed in, we were exhausted and a little raw from the arguing. But you would never know it, because everything would look very nice, as long as you didn't peek in my bedroom closet.

When we visited other people's houses, I *did* peek sometimes, in closets and cupboards, wondering whether they had done the same thing we did before guests arrived or whether they lived in this state of order all the time. It was easy to tell the houses where they did. I had one friend in college who still *freaked out* if you set one toe on his mother's bright white living room carpet because you might mess up the vacuum lines and she would *know* you had been in there. And imagining living in a house like that, in a family like that, felt as foreign and fascinating as imagining living on the moon.

And so, even though we were super social and pretty spontaneous people, the very worst thing in the whole world you could do to my family was *a drop-in*. If you stopped by unannounced, we'd open the door and invite you in, and meanwhile the hot shame would creep up my mother's face, and I would feel it mirrored in my own, my heart pounding hard, both of us with smiles plastered on, awkwardly acting glad to see you, but after you'd leave my mother would sometimes break down and cry, and I would feel awash in humiliation. *What did they think of us, seeing the house this way?* And then we'd fight, and clean, and insist that next time we'd be ready.

It never once occurred to me that how things looked might not be as important to other people as it was to us, or that they might have grace for the situation, or that they were really there to see *us*, and not to inspect our house and how well or poorly it was kept. All that mattered was that we felt embarrassed and lesser, unworthy of having a guest, and desperately disheartened. *If only* we'd had a little lead time so we could've been *prepared*!

Jesus tells a parable (in Matt 25:1–13) that we have come to see as about being properly prepared. It speaks of ten bridesmaids, waiting with their oil lamps to escort the bridegroom to the wedding feast. It calls five of them "wise" and five of them "foolish." The wise bridesmaids plan ahead; they expect the unexpected—they bring along extra oil just in case the groom is delayed. The foolish bridesmaids take the bridegroom at his word and prepare only for what is expected. As a result, they run out of oil. They are foolish, evidently, because they didn't go above and beyond.

Lucky wise ones! Good thing for them that the bride-groom was only delayed as long as he was and not very much longer, or they would've been fools too! But here is our first delightful clue that Jesus is up to his para-digm-flipping, parable-telling shenanigans: "wise and foolish," "smart and stupid," "better and worse." These are way-of-fear categories. The kingdom of God is about God's generosity and God's forgiveness and God's ability to reconcile us and restore us and transform us, and never about how well we earn or how much we deserve what God provides.

So here they are—these foolish and wise ones, and it's their job to bring the light, to greet the groom when he comes, and to lead the way to the party. And some of them feel *pretty darn proud* of themselves, *pretty darn* wise, and others feel like total, utter fools; they've failed the job. Sure, he was delayed, but they were not ready for him when he came, and now their lamps have no oil. *Worthless! Can't even do the job that was given us to do!* Is there anything more humiliating than being caught looking so stupid?

So they ask the others to share with them. But the others say no—because if we know one thing in this accounting-system kind of life, it's that there is only so much to go around, and if we don't look out for ourselves we are doomed. So they do what is only smart and they keep their own oil. *Go buy some for yourselves!* they say.

But the Way of God is abundance and not scarcity. It's forgiveness, sharing, and welcome, not judgment, competition, and scorekeeping, so we know we're deep in Jesus's master storytelling clutches now.

Those foolish bridesmaids without enough oil head to a deserted market at midnight in desperate hopes of finding some oil for sale somewhere, and in the process, *they miss the bridegroom when he comes.* And when they finally do return—we aren't even told whether it's with oil or empty-handed, because, spoiler alert, it's not about the oil—the groom says, "I don't know you," and they are dismissed and don't make it into the wedding feast.

So *keep awake*, the parable says.

If I were to hear this parable through the filter of my childhood shame, it would say, *Be ready for the drop-in at any moment.* Never let your guard down for a second. Keep things immaculate at all times, don't step foot on the living room carpet, go above and beyond, because you never know when the guest of honor could show up. And what if he caught you with a sink full of dirty dishes and clean laundry piled all over the couch?

In my twenties I grew to love a family who loved the drop-in. They wanted people to stop by any time. And they were completely intriguing to me because they didn't need to have the house in perfect order to sit down and enjoy a cup of coffee with you. They had young kids, and in fact, the house was often a mess, but that didn't stop them for a second being present and hospitable, making you feel like the best part of their whole day just may be this moment when *you* dropped in. They were available to you, open-hearted, undistracted, and present. This was absolutely novel to me—I had never considered before that instead of being totally prepared, with the clutter hidden away, homemade muffins on the table, and fresh vacuum lines in the rug, hospitality could mean encountering another, seeing and hearing and welcoming another, meeting them just as they are and just as you are—however that is in the moment.

The Way of Fear is loud, and its voice is inside us as much as around us. It even shapes how we read and take in Scripture. In many ways, the church has fallen prey to the same anxiety that dictates everything in the world's accounting system. We've spent centuries, off and on, painting God with the brush of judgment and threat, to fit our way of competition and scarcity, until the good news of God's grace gets buried underneath layers of pressure and guilt and striving. *Do better, don't mess up, get it right, try harder, go above and beyond, or you will be left out of the party altogether, and it will be as though God doesn't even know you.*

The truth is, the parable stirs up all of these anxieties and then *doesn't say*, "Have it all together! Don't be caught unprepared!" It says, *keep awake.* Be available. Watch for Jesus; let him encounter you when he comes. It's not about how full your lamp is when the moment arrives, how together you've got things. If it were about the oil, the bridegroom would've said, *Oh, good, you found some oil after all. Come on in, then.* Or, *Sorry, no oil? You substandard lamp-bearers. What inferior, inadequate bridesmaids you've turned out to be, not keeping your lamps lit properly! You are not worthy to be in this party.* But instead he says, *Who are you? I don't know you. I came and you were not there to meet me.* It's not about the role. It's about the relationship.

So, hooray if you can be prepared when the drop-in happens, when the bridegroom arrives. More points for you—if you're keeping track of that sort of thing. But if you can't be prepared, for whatever reason, *be available anyway.* Be here. Let him see you as you are. Be ready to welcome Christ whether you are ready or not.

The truth is, we can only burn so long before we burn out. We can only wait so long before we get drowsy. We can only carry so much oil before we run dry. None of us can go above and beyond in perpetuity, be prepared for company at every moment, be ready to impress and perform at the drop of a hat. That is the opposite of a biblical, Sabbath, way-of-God, deepest-belonging kind of life.

We have *no idea* when God will show up. In fact, the truth is, *God shows up all the time*, every day, and more often than not, we miss it. We are not here.

In the middle of my writing a sermon the night before I was to preach it, my daughter had a nightmare. I left my work and went to sit with her, but she was too afraid to go back to sleep. I said a number of—I thought—helpful things, coached her through some techniques. They maybe helped a little, but there was no breaking the nightmare's hold. I was feeling the pull and pressure of a late-night sermon needing to be finished. But instead of saying, "I have to go back to work now, you'll be OK," I stayed put. I worked to calm my own anxiety and stay available to her. And if I had left, I would have missed when Jesus silently showed up, in the form of her big brother getting out of bed, coming into her room without words, carrying a speaker with a playlist of music he had made for her, and plugging it in beside her. I would have missed watching love cast out fear, right before my eyes. That did it—she went right to sleep.

Sometimes we have full lamps. We may be in a position to share and give, may be able to light the way for others. Other times we will have run out of steam or will be falling apart at the moment. And if that's the case, the *very worst* thing we can do is go running off to frantically patch together some futile way of *looking like* we have it all together. Instead, if we simply *be here now*, as we are, we will find ourselves met by Christ in ways we could not have anticipated. Frederick Buechner says, "A crucial eccentricity of the Christian faith is the assertion that people are saved by grace. There's nothing *you* have to do. There's nothing you *have* to do. There's nothing you have to *do*. The grace of God means something like: 'Here is your life. You might never have been, but you *are*, because the party wouldn't have been complete without you.'"[1] So, let's not miss the party.

There is an ancient and rich Jewish tradition, dating back to the second century, called midrash. Midrash is an exploring kind of storytelling that probes for meaning, invites engagement, and raises implications by imaginatively filling in the gaps of the story. Let's do a midrash of this story.

> The five bridesmaids who were there to receive
> the bridegroom entered the party, lighting the

---

1   Originally published in Frederick Buechner, *Wishful Thinking: A Seeker's ABC* (New York: HarperOne, 1993), 34, and later in *Beyond Words: Daily Readings in the ABCs of Faith* (New York: HarperOne, 2004), 139.

way, and the crowd followed behind, laughing and dancing and making merry. When they arrived inside the courtyard, they saw, spreading out in every direction, tables, beautifully covered in colorful linens and set with sparkling dishes. Beyond that was a huge room—with a long banquet table heavy with delicious foods, a shining dance floor flanked by musicians, and an air of anticipation, abundance, and joy all around.

The crowd streamed through the courtyard toward the food and dance floor. But before they could go any further, the door matron stopped the bridesmaids. "You can't bring your lanterns in there," she said.

"Why?" one of the bridesmaids asked her. "We have an essential role to play!"

The door matron chuckled. "Oh, no, no. Your role is over. The only way to be in this party is to be a guest."

"But we've trimmed our lamps, and we have extra oil!" the bridesmaid protested. "Our light is what got the bridegroom here!"

The one standing next to her, nodding furiously, sputtered, "And how will people know we are the bridesmaids if we aren't holding our lamps?"

The door matron held up her hands and gently answered, "Listen, dears, here we have torches and chandeliers, fireflies in jars, bonfires, and candles on every surface—more light than we need, truth be told. There is nothing for you to do, no role to fill, no job to attend to, no place to earn. You are simply and entirely a guest, like everyone else here. Just find a comfortable seat and enjoy the music! Fill a plate and eat! Get out on the floor and let loose! That's all there is to it!"

She continued, "You did your part to celebrate the bridegroom's arrival! I get it. Great job!" Then she leaned toward them with a loud whisper, "But you do know that he would've found the front door anyway, right? Those lamps are mostly symbolic."

She gestured to the edge of the yard. "Please extinguish your lamps and place them in the dirt there, by the outer wall, to cool off. We'll douse them with water to speed the process along. Now, where is the rest of your group? There are supposed to be ten of you. . . ."

This life is not a competition. And it's not a solo act. There is enough light to lead the way for each other; there is enough light to welcome the bridegroom all together. Even if all of our lamps were to go out—Jesus is the light of the world! And we need only be here to receive the light, available to the moment of transcendence when it arrives. Light or no light, stockpiled goodness or bone dry and exhausted, wise or foolish in the world's eyes, overly prepared or desperate, however you are, just be here, right where you are, wherever you are. Here, now, is only place the God who comes near can meet you.

FOUR

Resting: Being Free

I am a multitasking ninja. If there were multitasking Olympics, I could compete. I can expertly juggle a balancing act with all my irons in the fire while keeping plates spinning. According to family lore, my grandfather could "fit ten pounds in a five-pound box." I am his legacy. But this performance goes on only so long until everything crashes and I have to pick myself up, brush myself off, and start all over again. And then my own body puts the kibosh on this supposed superpower with an autoimmune disorder that can flare up when I'm under stress.

I've had to learn, and learn to respect, my own limits. I've discovered that while I can do many things at once, it is much harder for me to do just one thing. While I could stuff ten pounds (poorly) into a five-pound box, I struggle to put in just five pounds. Or even four pounds, with some margins and wiggle room. I need help stopping. I won't stop if it's up to me to choose it. I need to practice the way of being human that infants know: to sleep when I am tired and eat when I am hungry. Contrary to the messages around us, and even my own instinct, I need to see rest as an essential act.

Our relationship to rest is complicated. We need it (literally, we would die without it), we crave it, and we are terrified of it. That statement sounds extreme, but I stand by it. Because time is so limited and moving so fast, and our lives are measured by what we produce and consume, there are very few justifiable reasons to rest. We see rest as a luxury tantalizingly hanging out there for that someday moment when all the work is finally done—when all the appointments are made, the bills are paid, and the leaves are raked and bagged at the curb. We also see it as a sign of weakness, as something lazy, unmotivated people do. Rest is reserved for the sick, the utterly depleted, the elderly, the boring, for those "fighting" cancer or recovering from surgery. When we absolutely can't keep going, and we're forced to stop and catch our breath, we can *briefly* rest until we can amp back up again. Or we can rest if it's a limited part of a justifiable self-care plan designed to keep us at optimum high-functioning capacity.

Instead of seeing time as something that holds us, we see time as something we can control, a commodity to be spent, wasted, maximized, and optimized. When we are feeling benevolent, we give people a temporary "needs rest" card on the board game of life, instead of recognizing that all species on the planet, and the very earth itself, require regular rest as integral to being alive. But usually, we view rest as something that takes us out of the fight, and that can make us feel like we're abandoning others. And if we rest too much, we're abandoning ourselves, violating the cultural mandate to *carpe diem*.

Our problem with rest is a symptom of our misconception of what is a good life. According to sociologist Hartmut Rosa,[1] our modern way of life is held together by what he calls "dynamic stabilization," which means we have created a system where we must constantly increase in order to merely maintain our position—increase speed, increase quantity, increase scope. We tell ourselves that the more

---

1   Hartmut Rosa is author of *Social Acceleration, A New Theory of Modernity, Resonance: A Sociology of Our Relationship to the World*, and *The Uncontrollability of the World*. You can read all about his work and the implications for ministry in the brilliant Andrew Root's superb Ministry in a Secular Age series.

we have, the more we know, the wider our reach, the more possibilities and opportunities at our fingertips, the freer and happier we will be. We believe that a good life is a life that is always reaching for more.

Rosa assures us this perspective is based not simply on greed; it is founded on fear. The world is moving so fast that we fear falling behind. If we don't keep up, if we don't keep increasing our reach, we will be lost. Never mind that some things can't speed up or increase. Some things have natural limits or can't be rushed, like the slow work of democracy, the pace of the earth itself, or the speed limit of the human soul.

To imagine stepping out of the pounding race and sitting down for a moment can feel terrifying. Not only will you surely lose your place and never catch up, but you're likely to get stepped on or kicked. Admitting you need rest—or, even worse, choosing to rest preemptively or regularly—is like admitting you are weak, just a human being and nothing more. And so we are. Resting means receiving our vulnerability. It acknowledges that just like all embodied creatures, we are nothing more than, or less than, alive.

Our faith story offers competing definitions of a good life. The first story of Scripture reveals humanity's origin as one of blessing, abundance. Resting is at the center of the life of the Trinity—simply being, belonging, abiding. Then God acts, bringing all into being from nothing. Again and again we read, "God saw that it was good. And there was evening and there was morning, a new day." And then, when creation is complete, God rests and enjoys what God has made. "Thus the heavens and the earth were finished, and all their multitude. And on the seventh day God finished the work that he had done, and he rested on the seventh day from all the work that he had done. So God blessed the seventh day and hallowed it, because on it God rested from all the work that he had done in creation" (Gen 2:1–3).

God also makes resting and enjoying not only part of the act of creation but integral to the identity of those made in the image of a God who both acts and rests. God begins the world with three blessings—a blessing of creation (Gen 1:22), a blessing of humanity (1:23), and a blessing of rest itself (2:3). And with the Sabbath command to rest (Exod 20; Deut 5), God invites human beings (what Karl Barth calls "seventh-day creatures") into this rest alongside the Creator, as creatures who care for creation and who also rest and enjoy the world with God. A good life is a life of belonging—caring for and enjoying one another and creation, and resting with God. This is humanity's purpose and how we experience our aliveness.

The second story of humanity reveals a contradictory definition of a good life. It is the story of the human drive to extend our reach. God tells the humans they are free to eat from the fruit of any tree in the garden except for one: the tree of the knowledge of good and evil. *Even though God said if you eat of this tree and you will die,* said the tempter, *really, you will be like God, knowing good and evil.* So they eat, and their eyes are opened to their vulnerability. They see their own nakedness and they cover themselves.

And here is the story of our sin. In a violation of the relationship between Creator and created, humans act as though they do not belong to God or to each other. They set the terms for their existence instead of accepting the identity God gives them—beloved humanity, cared for by God. They seek to transcend the boundaries of their own limitations and become like God. And when God comes to abide with them in the garden, the humans, aware of their nakedness, are afraid and hide from God.

In the beginning of the human story, we already see humans wanting to be more than we are, do more than we can, transcend our limits, and extend our reach. This description is nearly word for word Walter Brueggemann's definition of multitasking, "the drive to be more than we are, to control more than we do, to extend our power and our effectiveness. Such practice yields a divided self, with full attention given to nothing."[2] And when the first humans follow *this* definition of a good life, humanity gets its first taste of fear, shame, self-loathing, division, and blame.

Along with the commands not to murder or steal, God's command to regularly stop and rest is essential to upholding our humanity. What we have, what we do, what we make, or what we present to the world is not who we are. When we rest, our *doing* stops dominating us, and what arises is our being. Rest invites us to receive again our true identity as beloved, as beings cared for by God, and our true calling to minister as God does by caring for and enjoying one another and creation.

I love that in Jewish practice, the day, and so the Sabbath day, begins at sundown. As soon as the sun hits the horizon, what is done is done, and what is undone stays undone. There is no "finishing up" first; you simply start. Or rather, stop. This rhythm means that rather than rest being a reward for a job well done, or a last-ditch attempt to recover from hard labor or relentless racing, *rest is where it all begins.* There is evening and there is morning. A new day.

When the pandemic first hit and everything screeched to a halt, we felt the invitation of rest in ourselves and saw it in the world. When some people's lives ramped into high gear in order to keep things afloat for everyone else, we called them essential workers and showered them with gratitude. The rest of humanity was forced to stop doing all the things we were accustomed to doing. Meanwhile, in the absence of human noise and traffic, dolphins swam in the

---

2   Walter Brueggemann, *Sabbath as Resistance: Saying No to the Culture of Now* (Louisville: Westminster John Knox, 2014), 67.

Venice canals, lions sunned themselves on South African roads, the clouds of pollution lifted off cities in India and Italy, and Mount Everest was visible from Kathmandu, Nepal, for the first time in decades. It was a nod toward the imagined experience in Pablo Neruda's beautiful poem "Keeping Quiet," where he envisions a moment when the whole world simultaneously pauses its work and war: "we would all be together / in a sudden strangeness."[3] When so many people were forced to stay home, some slept more, or called loved ones for long conversations, or took meandering walks around their neighborhoods. In the pause of the noise, the world began speaking again, and for a brief moment, more of us were listening.

But accepting the rest was hard. Why not maximize this downtime and learn a new language? Become an expert in sourdough baking? Tackle that home improvement or self-improvement project? We got impatient with the slow pace of fighting a global pandemic. We got tired of being stuck within uncomfortable limits. We forgot—or worse, we turned on—our essential workers, whose exhaustion compounded. And when the restrictions lifted, before long we were racing to "catch up for lost time," and the lessons learned from the giant pause were mostly quickly forgotten.

"You have made us for yourself, O Lord, and our hearts are restless until they rest in you," St. Augustine said.[4] Like sleep, inspiration, or desire, we can't *make ourselves* experience rest, however. Even in the most "restful" circumstances, we can be anxious, preoccupied, and striving, resisting the invitation to belong to and abide with God and others. Stopping our activity and ceasing our work

----

3   Pablo Neruda, *Extravagaria: A Bilingual Edition*, trans. Alastair Reid (New York: Farrar, Straus & Giroux, 2001), 26.
4   Augustine, *Confessions* 1.1.

can't force us to be open to moments of transcendence or connection, but it can make space for them to happen.

The purpose of Sabbath time, the reason to keep sacred time, is to return to the ground of our being. To be. That this is difficult reveals how very necessary it is. That we will most often wonder whether we are *doing it right* indicates how addicted to *doing* we are. There is no one right way to keep Sabbath time. There are lots of great suggestions and ideas for what to *do* with the time, but the important thing is not what we *do*. It's that we stop *doing* long enough to just *be*. To be human. To be vulnerable before God and with our own selves the way that we really are. To listen to the sounds both outside and inside ourselves. To be alive.

In modern, optimized, controlled time, focused on doing more and having more, everyone always strives as though our very lives depend on it. But in God's Sabbath time we all simply are. The human categories of value and rank and comparison—like rich and poor, sick and well, old and young—are silenced. In shared humanity at rest, what speaks is the truth that we are all beloved humans made in God's image, and we are alive.

But we don't have shared humanity at rest. In our way-of-fear economy, we view even *rest* as a commodity to be distributed, bestowed, hoarded, or withheld. "No rest until there is justice" is a civil rights–era rally cry I hear often repeated today in the ongoing work for the real reality to be made manifest among us. But I realized recently that I hear this through modern ears—shaped by our individualistic, consumer, internet reality—as a call for tireless work, unceasing demands, the call for individual human beings to be the engine that brings about justice, which means that we must never stop, never rest. I long to hear "no rest until there's justice" with the eschatological imagination that Martin Luther King Jr. preached when he said, "The arc of the moral universe is long, but it bends toward justice."[5] We can participate in the justice that God is bringing.

"No rest until there is justice" is not a rally cry to mobilize the troops for unrelenting battle. It is a proclamation, a statement of fact, an indictment on our collective life in society. We cannot be a people at rest until there is justice. And justice manifests as rest for all. So, it's helpful for me to reverse it in my head: "No justice until there is rest." Because resting affirms we are human, *real justice is rest for all*. If we really lived like we belong to each other, we would all stop so all could stop. Therefore, our eschatological imaginations[6] compel us to come alongside those in our lives and communities who are facing a crisis, caring for someone chronically ill, or living with more responsibilities, fewer resources, more mouths to feed, and less backup support, and ask, *How can we practice belonging to each other with you? How can we care for each other so that everyone can rest?*

Different lives have different levels of busyness. And inside our own one human life, each of us experiences busy times and less busy times. Having young children in the house makes for a pace of life completely different from when they are grown and gone, for example. We live through chapters when we are more or less productive, more or less focused on building up or letting go. We face times of crisis that thrust on us greater obligations and responsibilities. Alternately, we get sidelined by things like job loss, surgery, retirement, or unexpected life changes and find ourselves with vast, uncomfortable swaths of unscheduled time when the last thing we feel like we need is more rest. But the point of Sabbath rest is not to improve at or

5   Martin Luther King Jr. was fond of quoting this aphorism first spoken by the early nineteenth-century preacher Theodore Parker.

6   See Root, *Deepest Belonging*, chap. 27, "Imagining: Living Now What Will Be."

have more of Sabbath rest. The point is to release us from that measure, return us to our life of belonging to God and each other, and remind us that we are not defined any way other than as beloved children of God.

Resting is practicing trust in God. Setting down our doing and sinking into our source. Surrendering our being into the resting being of the Divine to be held in the love that holds the whole universe together. I have begun to recognize that when I think I am least able to take a break is the time I most need to stop. Thinking I cannot stop is a flashing red warning signal to me that I am reaching beyond my limits, trying to be more than a vulnerable human being loved by God alongside all others. And I have stopped receiving my life, with my limits, as a gift. Inside my limits, my capacity to be truly alive is vast and expansive. But when I seek to transcend my limits, my soul atrophies, my relationships suffer, and I've stopped trusting God to be God and begun behaving as though the world can't run without Almighty Me.

Sabbath is God's gift to remind us whose we are and who we are. We are made in the image of a God who rests, belonging in a world that rests, called to be people who rest. And so we are alive. These beautiful, limited lives of ours are given to be received.

FIVE

Prayers for Receiving What Is

JESUS'S WORDS TO YOU—A BLESSING

My child . . .
I celebrate with you your accomplishments and your
    successes,
But if not a single one of them existed
I love you.

I grieve with you your failures and your frustrations,
But if they were the full sum of your actions in the
    world
I love you.

I know you completely. I'm proud of who you are.
You are one of billions who came before you
    and many more to come.
You are the only you that ever has been or ever will be.
I love you.

You are mine. And I love YOU.
You are not what you've done.
You are not what you've left undone.
You are nothing that you have built.
Nothing that you made in the world will last.
It will not remain.
But I remain.
And in my love, you remain.
When you move about in the world,
    you move in that love.
When you sleep, you sleep held in my love.
No matter where you are or what you are doing,
    you are my beloved child.

So you are free.
Free to risk. Free to try. Free to fail.
Free to grow. Free to fall. Free to love.

Held in my love, you are free to be *for life*.
This life and life everlasting.
I love you.

BE HERE NOW—A PRAYER OF PRESENCE

"Give your entire attention to what God is doing right
now, and don't get worked up about what may or may not
happen tomorrow. God will help you deal with whatever
hard things come up when the time comes." (Matt 6:34
The Message)

Be here now, O my soul.
Be here now, O my God.
May I be.

Just as I am without pretense or fear.
May I be here.

No other place my mind wants to take me.
Not work or the worries of family or friends,
not what I have to do or where I need to go.
Just here. Right here.

No other time my mind wants to take me.
Not past, for regrets or nostalgia,
and not future, for worry or planning or dreaming.
Just now. Right now.
May I be here now.

I trust you with this world and all those in it.
(Lift up specific prayers.)
Thank you, God.

I trust you with those I love and all they are going
through.

(Lift up specific prayers.)
Thank you, God.

I trust you with my own soul, all that I carry, and all
    that I am.
(Lift up specific prayers.)
Thank you, God.

Of all life and being, you are God.
In every place, you are God.
In every moment, you are God.

You are here now, God.
I am here now.
Let it be so.
Amen.

A PRAYER FOR THE MOMENT

Thanks be to you, O God,
for the gift of being alive.
Thank you that I am here.
Right now. This singular moment.

In the midst of my nonstop life,
of schedules, appointments, and tasks,
let me receive my life,
the whole of it,
the now of it,
the gift of it.

Let me be fully in my moments,
for instance,
this one,
right now,

recognizing every right now
for what it is:
a Spirit-soaked stage,
on which my life unfolds,
in which my soul exists,
my body moves,
my mind sparks and heart feels,
my love expands and connects,
with other
moving bodies, sparking minds, feeling
    hearts, and living souls,
one humanity
inside God's time.

I am alive.
I am part of Life.
Thanks be to God.
Amen.

PRAYER OF HEART WELCOME

I come to you this day, God, with my heart open.
I do not hide (nor could I)
any of my thoughts or feelings from you.

When fear would have me hide,
please help me show up.

When worry would have me distracted,
please help me return my mind and heart to you.

You are with me always.
You are with me now.
(pause)
Give me courage this day.

I trust you with my joy and my peace;
all contentment and harmony come from you and
    lead me to you.

I trust you with my sorrow and my anger,
even when my sadness or rage is toward you,
    God.

I trust you with my restlessness and discontent,
and allow myself to wonder what your Spirit might
    be stirring in me.

I trust you with my longings and my dreams;
you who made my imagination delight in it and
    meet me there.

I trust you with my questions and my doubts,
for by them you draw me deeper into life, closer to
    your heart.

May I remember this today:
You welcome me as I am.
You meet me in all of it.
May I welcome you and be present to you
in all things this day, O Christ.

And may I welcome myself today,
as you welcome me and are present with me
in all things this day, O Christ.
Amen.

PRAYER OF ATTENTION

"Search me, O God, and know my heart;
    test me and know my thoughts." (Ps 139:23)

What is arising in me, Lord?
This fatigue, this sadness, this joy, this wondering?
What are these tears releasing?
What is this laughter loosening?
Where am I in need? Where am I content?
What is shifting in me, Lord?
What is shutting down? What is opening up?
What is awakening? What is resting?
Where am I grieving? Where is my delight?
(Scan your heart and mind. Scan your body. Acknowl-
    edge what arises.)
Help me be present, O Christ, in all things,
As you are present with me now.
Amen.

PAUSE ME, ETERNAL ONE—A PRAYER

Pause me, eternal one,
in this moment. Just here.

My lungs fill with air,
my feet meet the ground
and stay. Steady. Still.

You are here, God.
I am here, God.

My heart beats and I notice it.
My mind clenches and sighs,
now at rest.

I am in in the world. Alive.
I am in your hands. Loved.
Thank you.
For life, for all.
Amen.

YES AND NO: PRAYER FOR A DAY OF REST

Today I will say Yes.
I will receive the life I have been given,
and accept the limitations and perimeters
within which I am me.
I will embrace the life that I am living,
and welcome the connections and possibilities
offered this day to me.
Today I will be guided by gratitude,
fed by fulfillment,
and moved by joy.
I will celebrate that I
have enough, am enough, and do enough.
And I will rest.

Today I will say No.
I will value my gifts,
care for my soul,
and stay open to God,
connected to other people,
and awake to this world's beauty.
Today I will trust that I am living my
    one life,
my purpose, my energy, and my joy
as faithfully as I can.
And if I am not,
I will say No to something
to make room for the Yes that will
bring me back to my true self and calling.
And I will rest.

Today, I give thanks
that in this universe of abundance and diversity,
my Nos free up others' Yeses,

and my Yeses support others' Nos,
because we all belong to each other,
and we all belong to God.
Today my life and choices will
contribute to justice,
enable freedom,
and support rest
in the lives of others.
Today I will live attuned to God,
attentive to those whose paths I cross,
and alive to the inner voice of my own soul,
and I will rest.

Guide my Yes and No today, Holy One,
and give me your rest.
Amen.

PRAYER OF REORIENTATION FOR WORK ROOTED IN REST

"If God doesn't build the house,
    the builders only build shacks.
If God doesn't guard the city,
    the night watchman might as well nap.
It's useless to rise early and go to bed late,
    and work your worried fingers to the bone.
Don't you know he enjoys
    giving rest to those he loves?" (Ps 127:1–2
        The Message)

The temptation is great, Lord, to jump into action.
My to-do list is long, my obligations this day are
    plenty.
May I be led

not by my own desires,
not by the demands of others,
not by the world's pressures and expectations,
nor even my job's,
but only by you.

By serving you alone,
I will share in the work that you are doing
in the lives of others,
and in the church and world that you love.
But if it becomes about me
—my strength, my ingenuity, my efforts—
then I am taking over your job,
for which I am woefully underqualified.

May your Spirit who hovered over the waters of
        creation
hover over me this day.
May nothing I do today come from my own striving,
but from your abundant life in me and your Spirit
        moving through me.

When I lose sight of you,
help me return to my starting point.
Begin me again where the day begins—in rest and
        trust.
That all I do today may flow
not from my full agenda, fragile ego, or lofty goals
but from the energy of your Holy Spirit.

God, I place in your highly capable hands . . .
(Lift up the needs, hopes, griefs, and longings of your
        own life, those you love, the ministry you share in,
        and the world.)

"Find rest, O my soul, in God alone.
My hope comes from God" (Ps 62:5 NIV modified).
Amen.

A PRAYER OF INTENTION FOR SABBATH TIME

Today is a Sabbath day.
For this day we will be conscious of *who we are*:
We will do things from joy rather than obligation.
We will notice what we need, and listen.
We will play, and rest,
and resist the urge to measure ourselves by what we
  accomplish.
Instead we will seek to simply be.
Beloved and free.

For this day we will pay attention to *whose we are:*
We will notice and reject the voices
that call us against or apart.
We will be gentle with ourselves
when those voices come from within.
We will release anxiety
and rest in trust.
Again and again.

For this day we will remember:
We belong to God, and we belong to each other.
To everyone everywhere.
Today we choose to celebrate that belonging
in whatever ways it occurs to us
whenever they arise.

God is right here.
Right.
Here.

Now.
It is all gift.

Today we stop
on purpose
to receive the gift.
This is the day that the Lord has made.
Let us rejoice and be glad in it.

SIX

Practices for Receiving What Is

LITURGY OF THE CELL PHONES

A liturgy for collecting or turning off cell phones. (Words of the people in bold.) To use in a secular setting, remove the last (italics) line of each movement.[1]

Prayer for Releasing Phones

We surrender our phones
to acknowledge that we are not as essential
as we would have ourselves believe
and to recognize how essential we are
to this moment, this conversation, this process.

We put down our phones
to put down the false belief
that we can be more places than here,
> **doing more things than this,**
and to commit to being fully present, here and
> **now.**

We turn off our phones
to turn to each other and to the moment at
> **hand,**
with full attention, creativity, and welcome.
May we receive the gifts of full presence and
> **essential connection.**
May God meet us in this moment.
Amen.
(Cell phones are shut down and surrendered.)

---

1   More than anything else I've written, this little liturgy has found a life of its own in the world.

Prayer for Retrieving Phones

> We return from this moment, taking with us the
>   gift of being fully present.
> **May we return with gratitude and perspective**
> **to the tasks before us and the noise around us,**
> **a little more willing to resist the urgency,**
> **and a little more able to receive the quiet gifts**
>   **of each moment**
> *where God is present alongside us.*
> **Amen.**
> *(Cell phones are reclaimed.)*

JUST YOU—A WALKING PRAYER

Walking In
> Pause at the beginning of your walk.
> Before you begin, imagine you are setting down
>   at the start all your accomplishments, your
>   goodness, even your burdens. Envision
>   dropping them around you.
> Step out of them and step into this walk with
>   God into the center of your vulnerable self.
>   Here is just you—your pure essence, your
>   core self, where you and God are together.
> Listen with your being as you walk slowly in.

The Center
> Rest in the center in God's love.

Walking Out
> Let God's love guide you out.

BELONGING—A WALKING PRAYER

Walking In
  As you walk, let your mind relax.
    When thoughts come in, greet them and let
    them go ("I'll think about you later!"). Feel your
    body move; feel your breath go in and out. Let
    yourself be present right here and now. God is
    with you.

The Center
  When you reach the middle, stay there and think
    of one experience this week when you felt your
    belonging to God or your belonging to the human
    family. When did you experience resonance or
    aliveness? Connection? Life?

Walking Out
  When you're finished with the memory, walk back out.
    Let yourself rest in gratitude and trust that God
    is with you now. If you don't feel that, that's OK.
    However you walk, just be present with God.

AVAILABILITY—A JOURNALING PROMPT

When in my life right now am I most available to God?
When am I least available to God?[2]

ABIDING WITH GOD—A JOURNALING PRAYER

Take a piece of paper and a pen/pencil.

Write at the top of the page "God."
  Sit quietly until your spirit begins to speak to God's Spirit.

---

2   Thank you to Julie Neraas for this question.

Begin writing.
>When you reach the end of what you've written, wait and see whether there is more.

When you are finished, turn over the paper and write your own name on the top.
>Listen. Wait.
>Let yourself write God's response to you.

ABIDING WITH GOD—A WALKING PRAYER

>Before you begin to walk, pause and say to God, aloud or in the silence of your heart, "Hi." When you feel you are here and you've acknowledged God is here, Begin to walk.

>Walking In
>>Walk slowly. Maybe try matching your breath to your feet. Listen. When your mind wanders, invite yourself back to this moment where God already is by again saying to God, "Hi."

>The Center
>>Rest in the center with God.

>Walking Out
>>Walk out with God.

ABIDING WITH GOD—A PRAYER FOR OTHERS

>*This is a good prayer for not telling God what to do or turning fretting into "praying."*[3]

>Simply say the following prayer to God.

---

3   I'm grateful to Rev. Kristen Jeide for teaching our congregation how to pray in this way.

Insert a name, and then rest in that prayer.
Repeat with other names as desired.

> Here now
> with you
> for _____.

ABIDING WITH GOD—A PRAYER PRACTICE FOR THE WORLD

Choose a place in the world to pray for.
> Use some symbol for that place—pulling up a picture of a map or its flag on your phone, using an image from the news or an item from the country—as a way to focus your attention.

Ask God to show you how to pray.

Listen with your heart.
> Listen on behalf of the people in that place, on behalf of the land, animals, and ecosystem of that place. Let your heart and imagination open up. Invite the Holy Spirit to let you share in God's heart for that place. No words are necessary. Your prayer may be just a feeling.

Let yourself be here, with God, on behalf of these others.

GOD'S PRESENCE, THEIR PRESENCE—A PRAYER FOR OTHERS

As you pray for others, instead of begging God to intervene—which is an important and legitimate way to pray—this time try praying with a sense that God is already there, already at work in their lives.

Light a candle for the person.

> Hold the candle and imagine it as their unique life, shining in the world. God is holding them; they are held in God. God is already loving and caring for them, even if you can't see it.

Pray for the person in a spirit of gratitude instead of worry.

> Hold that inner stance as you think of that person.

When you are finished, thank God for the blessing this person is in the world and for God's presence already with them.

NIKSEN—A SABBATH PRACTICE

The Dutch concept *niksen* literally means "to do nothing," "to do something without any purpose or aim at all." It doesn't matter what you do, or even for how long you do nothing.

To practice *niksen*, just let yourself do nothing. Gaze out the bus window, turn off the radio in traffic and just be. Sit in a quiet room of your home before anyone else is awake. The point is that there is no point, no intention to be productive in any way or accomplish anything at all. Just be idle.

If it helps, you can set a timer. You can expect discomfort. This is normal. We are used to doing; doing makes us feel good. We're pretty terrible at just being, and just being without doing can make us feel pretty terrible at first. Notice the discomfort and offer it to God. Stay with it, and it will diminish.

This is the most basic form of humanity: being. In God's presence. No agenda (not even trying for awareness that you're in God's presence). Simply being.

AIRPLANE MODE: PACING—A SABBATH PRACTICE

By Becca Dean, a friend and professor at Ridley College, Cambridge, who recently shared with me her experience with myalgic encephalomyelitis or ME (aka chronic fatigue syndrome) and a specific therapy called "pacing" that was prescribed to her. This practice is modeled after that experience, taking the above concept of niksen a bit further, with her instructions.[4]

A Daylong Pacing Practice
> In a twenty-four- or forty-eight-hour period, stop any activity whatsoever every forty-five minutes and

....

4   Becca shares, "In 2013 I became ill with what was later diagnosed as ME. Chronic fatigue syndrome gives a bit more sense of what it's like but still skims the surface of how drastically my life was disrupted and transformed by this illness. Over a couple of months I went from having the energy of a super-human twenty-six-year-old who went running between meetings to relax, to someone who was not well enough to walk down stairs.

"In time, I was given some support to manage the illness and was put on a 'pacing' regime. I hated it. It was a drastic response to a drastic condition. I wanted my old life back, and this felt like conceding to something that could be long term.

"At first it was awful. It felt like being even more removed from the world that I was already struggling to live in. And forced isolation was harrowing. Without any distraction my fears and grief got louder. I had a distressing few days getting used to it. And then, like the moment a plane makes it through the grey and bumpy clouds, light and peace met me. God was there, and my fifteen minutes became Holy Ground—like living with one foot on earth and another in heaven. I got peaceful. I felt utterly beloved and held. I no longer needed to keep up with everyone because the time away had become transfigured, luminous.

"I don't pace like this anymore, but I do still pace. I have lost that sense of deep connectedness with God. But my mind, body, and soul remember now how to rest in God's presence. The more often I do it, the more I want to, the more I can't imagine why I don't! Befriending this silence has been one of the most transformative and empowering practices, and classically I went into it kicking and screaming!"

rest in utter inactivity for fifteen minutes. Imagine you are putting yourself on airplane mode at the end of every hour. Activities to cease include conversations, watching TV, listening to the radio, standing up, or walking. Fifteen-minute blocks are for silence, sitting or lying down, and if possible removing yourself from the company of others.

Pacing Three Times a Day

Three times a day—once in the morning, once in the afternoon, and once in the evening—take yourself away to somewhere where you can "just be"—a bedroom, a sofa, a coffee shop, or a bench. Set a timer for fifteen minutes, so you don't watch the clock. Put your phone on airplane mode. It may take a while to settle, so try to redirect your wandering mind when you notice that you're worrying or thinking about what you have to do next. Mull over your belovedness, putting yourself in God's gaze, and putting your gaze on a God who is present to you even when you're unaware.

SETTING SABBATH INTENTIONS—A LITURGY FOR RESTING

This liturgy can be done alone or with others for a day you intend to set aside for Sabbath practice. This can be done at the beginning of the sabbath day, or even the night before.

Sit down before the day begins and imagine that you are making a pact with God, yourself, and your people. You are saying, *Today I will live in awareness and presence, awake to God, myself, and others.* The joy of Sabbath days is letting things unfold as they will—paying attention to what you need in the moment and responding. Having intention at the outset can help you be more conscious that throughout the day that you are making choices.

On this day, you are saying yes to some things—by choice or by accident. And by default, you are saying no to other things, and that can be on purpose too. This is one small way to practice yes and no, to get used to how they feel in our mouth and our bodies.

Write YES or NO at the top of a paper and draw a line in between them.

Then ask yourself, or one another, two questions:
1. What do you want to say yes to today to remember who and whose you are?
2. What do you want to say no to today to remember that you are free?

Or sometimes, it can be more fruitful to reverse the questions:
1. What do you want to say no to today to remember who and whose you are?
2. What do you want to say yes to today to remember you are free?

Some things you might think of immediately, such as saying no to email, social media, or screens in general. But maybe you need to say no to driving, returning phone calls, or social obligations. Or maybe you need to say yes to getting together with friends or calling someone you've lost touch with, napping, creative or artistic endeavors, cooking (or *not* cooking—preparing food the day before and having it ready), getting outside into nature. Let yourself imagine what the gift of a whole day for the needs of your soul might look like, and then set the perimeters.

Make your YES and NO lists.

Return to them as needed throughout the day.

RECEIVING WHAT IS

BACK-TO-SCHOOL BLESSING

Invite the children, teachers, and parents of your congregation or in your family to share a symbol of the upcoming school year and pray this blessing over them.

Pencils, backpacks, lunch boxes, and folders—
we lift to you the tools of this school year.
They represent the learning we will be doing,
and the places and ways we will be doing this
    learning.
As we hold in our hands these tools,
and hold in our hearts this school year,
we ask your blessing on us, Gracious One.

May our teachers teach with wisdom, grace, imagi-
    nation, and love.
Give them patience and gentleness with themselves
and their students.
Mark out for them the times to work and the times
    to rest.
And give them joy in their teaching.

May our learners grow in wisdom, grace, imagina-
    tion, and love.
Give them patience and gentleness with themselves
and their teachers.
Mark out for them the times to work and the times
    to rest.
And give them joy in their learning.

May our parents parent with wisdom, grace, imagi-
    nation and love.
Give them patience and gentleness with themselves
and with their children.

Mark out for them the times to work and the times
    to rest.
And give them joy in their parenting.

Lord, bless these students.
Bless these teachers.
Bless these parents.
Bless this learning.
May we remember education is not about memoriz-
    ing facts and figures.
It is about awakening our inspiration, expanding our
    horizons,
deepening our appreciation for living,
and expanding our capacity to participate
in a full life alongside each other.
Amen.

A GARDEN BLESSING

*This blessing uses a handful of soil, a container of water, and a
handful of seeds.*[5]

Blessing the Soil
(hold a handful of soil)

Origin of all life,
All we need for life you've given us. Everything
    works together:
ground and sky, air and water, insects and birds,
    animals and humans.

....

5   This prayer was written for the community of St. Joseph's Home for
    Children for the opening of their new garden, a ministry started by
    Chaplain Amy Teske, which eventually became a thriving community
    mission.

We all share this earth, each doing our part to care
for all the rest.
Thank you for the earth.
Bless this soil.
We thank you for all the miracles of life that will
happen within it
under the ground, in the darkness, hidden where we
can't see them.
Amen.

Blessing the Seeds
(hold a seed in your palm)

Creator of all Life,
You put into a tiny seed all the potential for a whole
new living thing.
But it doesn't grow on its own.
You provide sun and water, worms and bees, air and
earth.
And then you invite us to join in the process:
to plant and nurture, tend and harvest, eat and enjoy.
Thank you for the limitless potential inside some-
thing so small.
Thank you for the community that brings it to life.
Bless these seeds.
Bless them as they grow.
Amen.

Blessing the Water
(pour water on your hands)

Maintainer of all life,
You don't just start things and walk away,
set the world in motion and ignore it.
You keep providing.
Thank you for the amazing gift of water:

water that comes down from the sky and up the
    ground,
that flows in rivers and pools up in lakes, that fills
    vast oceans and our own bodies too,
water that refreshes our thirst, washes, and makes
    clean,
nourishes, and makes strong.
Bless the water
that will nourish this garden.
Bless the rain that will fall
and the hands that will pour it, providing, like you
    do,
for each growing thing.
Amen.

Blessing the Herb Garden
(taste some herbs)

Bless this herb garden and all it represents.
Thank you for life and the invitation it gives.
Bless these herbs
that bring flavor and brightness.
Thank you, Creative God,
    that you give us what we need,
but you also give more:
you fill life with spice and taste, aroma and zest.
Thank you for inviting us to be creative too;
to learn and uncover new flavors, to mix it all up in
    unique and exciting ways,
to welcome and appreciate all the deliciousness of
    life.
Amen.

PART TWO

Receiving What's Difficult

SEVEN

Repenting: Being Found

When I was in college, I spent the large part of a summer sleeping on a three-foot-round papasan chair cushion on the floor of an apartment five friends were renting in Dinkytown, near the U of M campus in Minneapolis. At one point, we ran out of toilet paper and went through all the napkins, coffee filters, and finally Far Side comics before someone finally bought more. But whatevs. We were young.

When Andy and I graduated from seminary in Los Angeles, we were in our mid-twenties and were willing to go anywhere in the United States to start our next life chapter. Coast? Desert? Mountains? Big city? Tiny town? Sure! Why not! Andy applied to graduate programs all over, and we ended up moving to Princeton, New Jersey, packing up all our things in a trailer and driving for five days across the country. We spent each day listening to Harry Potter CDs and eating sunflower seeds and drive-through fast food. Each night we strategically parked the truck with everything we owned in the world, towing our only car, where we could watch it from our motel window so it wouldn't get stolen.

There are times in our lives we anticipate upheaval. We expect it; invite it, even. We are totally open to change, happy to cooperate with a little chaos. But I think we think that is supposed to stop—that we go through our change-and-chaos phase, and then after that, things are supposed to be predictable and secure.

But the turmoil never stops, and upheaval is not an isolated incident. Children, or not, homes gained and lost, illnesses, adjustments—the changes just keep coming. That first friend to get divorced becomes one of many, maybe even yourself. That dream job you pursued falls through, that church you loved falls apart, that person you trusted falls away. And then they take your favorite show off the air, and stop making your favorite ice cream, and tear down your favorite local diner to put up another Starbucks. The president you loved is replaced by one you can't stand, and that woody place where you found silence and solace as a child has become a crowded, rowdy resort.

And instead of settling down, the changes seem to speed up. More friends move away, drift away, or pass away. Your doctor retires, and your phone becomes obsolete, and every ten years or so (my grandma once commented to me) your body seems to have become a completely different shape from the one you'd adjusted to and has added on to its ever-growing catalog of cricks and quirks. At sixty-two, you discover, a job loss is nothing at all like it is at twenty-two. And these are just the little changes, the everyday, ordinary, constant disturbances. These are to say nothing of global crises, natural disasters or community violence, catastrophes, misfortunes, life-altering diagnoses, and devastating deaths.

Disruption doesn't restrict itself to phases, and chaos doesn't play by any rules. Trouble, tumult, and seismic shifts happen in our lives and in the world *all the time*. From birth until death, living with the unexpected and navigating constant change is part of being human.

Also, part of being human is to try to diminish disorder. We like to pretend we have more control than we do. We mitigate risk and bolster security however we can. We depend on all sorts of things to make us feel safe and stable, because, as it turns out, we are dependent beings—we can't do this life thing all on our own. We need to find our strength and security somewhere.

So we rely on our intellect or our bank accounts, our health history and insurance policies. We trust institutions and governments, leaders, pastors, and teachers (or we don't, and instead we trust those who say not to trust them). We depend on the climate, community, and culture to give us predictable ways of living in the world, and then we act like they can't, or at least shouldn't, change. But they do. It turns out that none of these things, ultimately, can protect us. They can make us feel secure for a time, but anything can change at any moment.

So what are we to do?

The opening line of Psalm 46 sums up the theology of the whole Psalms in these words: "God is our refuge and strength." God is the One we are to depend on. God is our safety. "A very present help in trouble." Not a helper in the midst of trouble but Help itself. *Very present* help. Right here. Right now. Right in the midst of it. "Therefore we will not fear."

Therefore. Even though the earth changes. And mountains fall into the sea, and tsunamis and storms and whirlwinds roar through our world, and the very ground seems to shake beneath our feet, and turmoil and tumult overwhelm us. Even though. Not because these things don't or won't happen but because they will and do. Still. We will not fear. Why? Because God is our refuge, our strength, a very present help in trouble.

But how do we get from finding refuge in things that cannot protect us, depending on things that cannot save us, and trusting in things that cannot give us stability or meaning to finding refuge in, depending on, and trusting in God?

The one-word sermon of fiery street-corner preachers was a favorite of Jesus too. *Repent!* Jesus says, *for the kingdom of God has come near!* But *repent* does not mean "to

wallow in your disgustingness and come groveling
back to God." It means "turn around, change your mind,
look at things differently"! The Greek word for *repent*
means literally "change how you think after being with,"
that is, turn around, shift your being in another direction,
change your purpose after this encounter. In other words,
exchange your way of seeing for God's way of seeing. God's
reign and God's way are already unfolding among us. We
can trust this.

But giving up our way of seeing things is hard. And
trading our way of seeing for God's way of seeing the world
exposes the things we turn to for refuge from the tumult
of life that are not God. The flimsy, counterfeit security
we find in camping out with those who are just like us
and shutting out those we don't understand. The sense of
well-being we get from a well-paying job or a well-spoken
compliment. The measuring and comparing, *are we more
or less secure than those people are?* The soothing lies and
half-truths that ease our consciences or pacify our egos. The
protection we feel from nursing hatred, assigning blame,
and tending anger. We find refuge in all sorts of voices,
places, and things that cannot ultimately save us or make
us any safer or more whole. They mostly just make us more
trapped by the trouble we are seeking to escape. Repenting
turns us from those things back to our true source of life,
God.

And then, repenting leads to confession and forgiveness, or confessing and forgiveness lead us to repentance.
In either case, exchanging our way of seeing for God's way
causes us to recognize our sin, that is, the ways we have,
either on purpose or accidentally, put up barriers between
ourselves and God or others. Repenting and seeing things
from God's perspective instead of our own reveal where we
have brought pain, suffering, and harm on ourselves and
others, so that we can reach out for healing and forgiveness
and let God reconnect us to God and others.

But we tell ourselves that maybe we'll avoid trouble if we avoid repenting. If we hide our violations and our anxieties and move on, pretending we're secure, maybe that's almost as good as *being* secure. So we avoid seeing things from God's view because it could get us into trouble. We may have to confess. It might make us have to act differently. Did I say something about someone else that caused them embarrassment or pain? Am I cheating on my taxes or my spouse? Have I replaced rest with alcohol, Netflix, and Candy Crush to avoid having to be present with my discombobulated self? Who among us would jump at the chance to come clean about any of these things? Repent? That's just walking into trouble.

But this God of ours *is found* in trouble, is *very present* there, in fact! For those who've had trouble brought down on them by others, and those who bring trouble on themselves, God is Help itself. "God is our refuge and strength, a very present help in trouble."

We have no good human mechanism for getting ourselves out of sin, the power of sin, the mindset of sin, which is separation, isolation, judgment, fear. Paul says we are slaves to sin. Trapped in sin, we move to the punishment for sin: condemnation. Sin is living as though God is not God and we are not beloved children of God created to live with and for each other. So when we get caught in sin, and we are suddenly aware that we are caught in sin, we often sin more to try to make ourselves not feel so alone, so trapped, so disappointed in ourselves. Or we judge and condemn ourselves or one another for the sin, which is just another way of staying locked in sin, being ruled by the Way of Fear.

God's mechanism for getting us out of sin is repentance. Repenting is letting ourselves be found again. Like sunflowers turning their face toward the sun, like exhausted, angry toddlers running back into their parents' arms, repenting returns us to our true selves and our true place in God. We turn our wilting little hearts back toward their source of life, and in our lostness we are found. We don't even have to believe we will find mercy, though we will. We may be craving the judgment and condemnation we think we deserve. But this is the power and beauty of the way of God: once we repent, once we turn our sorry selves back toward love, we are released from judgment and condemnation. Once we repent, we absorb the grace that was always there and find ourselves held by God with others. We only need to trust just enough in that belonging to be open to being found, to being willing to have our way of being exchanged for God's way. Or maybe it's even more basic: we just need to admit we are lost to discover we are already found.

The exhausted Israelites living in exile in Babylon were ripped from home and stuck somewhere unfamiliar and uncomfortable that was not home. They were exhausted by turmoil, unsettled by circumstances, unsure of their capacity. They didn't know whether they had what it took to live up to their end of the deal. In fact, all evidence from history and experience told them that if it were up to them to remember their belonging and live from that truth, they would fail at staying true to God. But God said it was not their job to uphold this relationship.

In Jeremiah 31 the promise of the prophet to the people is that God will claim them as God's own, cover them in love and faithfulness, and provide for them in rest and abundance. Their relationship with God will not be dictated by rules or shaped by fear of punishment or demand careful tiptoeing. Instead, this connection will be defined by love, covered in grace, and secured by the Divine and not by them, a relationship steered by the One who anticipates their need for salvation and offers it before they ask. God will make a new covenant, a new bond, not dependent on their ability to remember correctly and teach each other rightly, but written into their very hearts, every one of them. This covenant can't be broken because it will be inside them, and God will do the heavy lifting. They will be secure in their belonging to God, and God will be the one who makes sure that's so. "I will put my law within them, and I will write it on their hearts; and I will be their God, and they shall be my people" (v. 33).

I long to be connected and alive, to sense God and see others. And I long to contribute to connection and love and joy for others. We are made for this, drawn to this: to live in belonging to God and each other. When this is severed, we are exiled from our true home. And when this bond holds, no matter where we are, we are at home. Repentance is the gift of this reconnection—being found again for this belonging. Repentance brings us home when we fall away, reminds us what's real when we forget, and allows us to be put back together again by God, whose love and mercy meet us not only when we step up and reach out but especially when we're stuck. God's goal isn't punishment but reconciliation, reconnection. God wants for us wholeness and love.

So we get to step up and claim it. We get to accept being accepted. Repentance is the wake-up moment when we say, *Oh! I want to trade my pitiful way of greed, resentment, and constant condemnation for God's way of love that connects me to God and other people!* And in that moment, God's salvation meets us exactly how we need to be met, to heal us where we are sick, and mend us where we are broken, and release us where we are caged, and find us where we are lost, to be our refuge in times of tumult. Our anger or disappointment, our mistakes or stupidity, the chaos around us or within us—these things do not get to set the terms, define our lives, keep us divided from each other, trapped in shame, or stuck in fear. God's love sets the terms. God's care holds us. God's grace claims us and restores us to trust in our connection to God and each other.

We will spend our energy trying to avoid, diminish, or escape trouble. When we repent, we find refuge in the God who is a very present help in the midst of trouble. We will seek to wall ourselves off ineffectively from chaos and guard ourselves unsuccessfully from weakness. When we repent, we rest our being in God, who is our strength and our refuge.

Therefore, we will not fear. Not because trouble doesn't find us or find others because of us. Not because the chaos dies down, or the earth remains tranquil, or our lives stay stable and unchanged, or we never mess up and cause pain and we always feel settled and secure. But because right in the midst of sin, trouble, chaos, change, mess-ups, and pain, God is our refuge and our strength. God finds us.

EIGHT

Praying: Being Honest

W hen amusement parks first reopened in Japan after
the Covid-19 pandemic lockdown, they had some
new rules. Hung where you could see it as you were board-
ing the roller coaster was a sign that read, "Please scream
inside your heart." I discovered it when someone shared it
in a tweet that said, "After six months, 2020 finally has its
motto."

Paul says in Romans 8:26–28 that in our weakness,
when we don't know how to pray, the Spirit intercedes for
us with groans too deep for words. In other words, when
we are screaming inside our hearts, we have a translator.

Maybe we've thought this means that when we're praying and we aren't using the right words, the Holy Spirit tells
God what we really mean. But the syntax indicates that it
actually means, when we *don't even know what it is that we
want*, let alone how to ask for it, the Spirit groans with us
and for us with a meaning known to God.[1] When we are
trapped in confusion and can't even identify what to ask
for, when we have no idea what would help and we are just
screaming inside our hearts, the Spirit intercedes, turning
our silent screams into prayers for exactly what God knows
we need.

This is such good news to me. Praying in times of
suffering or loss or upheaval or unknown is often hard.

---

1   According to James D. G. Dunn, "Spirit Speech: Reflections on
     Romans 8:12–27," in *Romans and the People of God*, ed. Sven K.
     Soderlund and N. T. Wright (Grand Rapids: Eerdmans, 1999), 89.

We like to tell God specifically what we want God to do for us. Usually when we pray, we give God a little direction. This isn't bad; it's just kind of cute. When my daughter was three years old, she would stand on a stool next to the counter, watching me intently. Pointing her little finger, she'd give me detailed, step-by-step instructions for how to make her toast. As she told me how to do it, she'd also patiently remind me how she'd prefer it to turn out (*lightly toasted, lots of butter, all the way to the edge, please*).

We pray like this, as though God is a mom who "needs" us to give her step-by-step instructions for how to do her job and who maybe has also forgotten our preferences and could use some helpful reminding of how we'd like it all to turn out. We tell God things like, "Please guide the surgeon's hands," "Help her feel better," "End the violence." And we pray for God to do the things God already does and be the things God already is. "God, bring your peace and comfort." "God, be with us here."

This is all just fine. There's nothing wrong with praying this way. (The Spirit translates these prayers too!) But sometimes, often, we ask way too small. We pray in a "help us get through this" kind of way, when what God may want to do is more of a "use this to completely transform everything" kind of thing.

The bottom line is, prayer is something we've made overly complicated, and God hears us however we ask and whatever we say. But I absolutely love that Paul is telling us we don't have to know what to ask for, and it's OK if we can't really find the words to *say* anything. We don't even have to know what we really want from God. We just have to scream inside our hearts. And with sighs too deep for words—at a frequency maybe our ears can't even hear—the Holy Spirit turns our silent screaming into prayer that God, who searches our hearts and knows the mind of the Spirit, hears and responds to.

I could stop there, and that would be enough. But it just keeps getting better. The next verse has been widely misunderstood and misused. "All things work together for good for those who love God." In utter contrast to what came just before it, this feels like a shushing of deep suffering. It sounds like a trite answer to silence the deep groaning and sighing that we have just been told the Spirit takes up on our behalf. And it feels exclusionary, like, *Hey, if you're someone who loves God and who's lucky enough to be called according to God's purposes, God will make sure everything that happens to you turns out good, so cheer up!*

But apparently our own human nervousness crept into the translations. The original Greek actually says something like, "In everything God works for the good, together with those who love God."[2] First of all, it tells us God is actively working in all things. Things themselves don't work together for good. It's not advocating an "everything will work out" approach to life. There is a distinct agent here, and it's God. In every situation, every moment, every conflict, and *especially* in suffering, God works persistently and unrelentingly toward healing and wholeness and connection.

And second, our part, then, is not to just cross our fingers, paste on our smiles, and pat each other's shoulders, saying, *One day this will feel better; God will make a bad thing turn out good, you'll see.* Our place is to join God where God is working, to work together *with* God for the good, because *with those who love God, God works in all things for the good.*

When we are screaming inside our hearts at our own pain and the terrible suffering and injustice in the world, we are working together with God. N. T. Wright says, "We

2 As explored in depth in Haley Goranson Jacob, *Conformed to the Image of His Son: Reconsidering Paul's Theology of Glory in Romans* (Downers Grove, IL: IVP Academic, 2018).

are being God-lovers, inspired by the Spirit to groan in such a way that God the heart-searcher knows what is going on. We are caught up in the love of God for the world, which is a painful love, because the world is in a mess."[3] God will work for the good. And we will join in at the very place of pain because that is where God's Spirit is working.

Not only is suffering "not worth comparing with the glory that is to come" (Rom 8:18), but suffering is something *through which God is bringing new life.* The cross reveals to us that in Christ God comes specifically *into* suffering. If you want to know where to find God, it's in suffering. Not just to share suffering, but to work in it and through it to bring new life. God brings life out of death. That's what God does. So we go to the death, and we wail there at the agony of it, with insistent, expectant waiting for God's new life to appear.

And we're told that when we do this, the Spirit—the same Spirit who hovers over the water at creation, whose breath becomes life in human lungs, who guides the people of God across the Red Sea and through the wilderness as a mighty pillar of fire at night and cloud by day to the promised land—that same Spirit is in us, groaning deeper than any of our words, for the salvation of the world, for an end to suffering, for the hope and promise of God to be fulfilled in our midst. Our crying out in places of suffering joins in God's work of redemption.

So here is what we will do: all the places of despair within us, and conflict between us, that rise in us like a silent scream, the pain we have no words for, we will turn toward those places of suffering instead of fleeing

---

3 Miroslav Volf and N. T. Wright, "N. T. Wright on Weeping, Waiting, and Working with God in the Pandemic," July 18, 2020, in *For the Life of the World*, produced by Yale Center for Faith and Culture, https://faith.yale.edu/media/n-t-wright-on-weeping-waiting-and-working-with-god-in-the-pandemic.

them. Racism, addiction, illness, broken ties, and broken futures—we will cry out about them. And we won't worry about trying to tell God what we think God should do to solve the world's problems, or even our own. Because our solutions will undoubtedly be too small and shortsighted anyway. We'd suggest repair and renovation to a God who specializes in resurrecting the dead.

So we'll let that pressure go—to solve it all for God, or to be strong prayer warriors, or even to have words. We'll go into our weakness, where we have no idea how to pray or what to do, and we'll just bravely wait there, with our screams and groans, sharing the heart of God and letting the Spirit translate it all into prayers for God to bring new life into our places of death. And then, in our giving, and loving, and marching, and listening, and seeking, and praying, and speaking out, and joining in, we will trust that we are working together with God for an outcome shaped not by our limited imaginations but by God's limitless love.

NINE

Narrating: Being Rooted

After George Floyd was killed, our city erupted in anguish. One morning, after a particularly difficult night, a member of my congregation, Andrea, texted me.

"I woke up to the smell of smoke from my open windows. At first I didn't know if someone had lit a bonfire or if it was coming from Lake Street. The more I read, the more likely it seems to be from Lake Street."

I couldn't respond. I was just then taking in the news from the previous night—the widespread destruction, the death, the unquenchable anger and sorrow, holding up Martin Luther King Jr.'s words, "Riots are the language of the unheard." We were watching our city wail. I felt unmoored by it. I tried to gather my thoughts to respond to her, but before I could type anything, she texted again,

"This is part of the story. This is not the whole story. The world belongs to God."

When I read this, I felt myself land. Physically, I actually felt a *ka-thunk* in my body. *Yes.* These are the words our congregation sent to each other on postcards, magneted to our refrigerators, taped on our bathroom mirrors and printed on lawn signs when the Covid-19 pandemic began. We put them where we could see them and remind one another, over and over. Her words brought me back. I was rooted again. I felt myself breathe again. I know this. I trust this.

We can look right at it all—and we should—and say, "This is part of the story." *Oh Lord, hear our prayer! God, have mercy!*

But we also say, "This is not the whole story." Because it isn't.

For the next few minutes, we found ourselves supporting each other, she and I. With humor, reminders of God's presence, dipping in and out of our morning routines, and with the deepest truth and last word: "The world belongs to God."

She said, "I keep looking at my backyard. It's so green. There are flowers everywhere and the peonies are starting to bud."

"And yet there is stench."

"The discord between the stillness and beauty and the faint but persistent smoke smell."

"The kids' toys are sort of strewn about the yard, which adds promise of movement."

"And then I smell smoke again."

I took it in. I breathed. It felt holy. "God, in your mercy," I responded.

Gratitude welled up in me. The moment felt sacred.

I had been seeking solutions, the right words, a place to stand, something to do, answers, a container for the confusing mix of emotions. And she gave me back the deep reminder and the holy work. "This is prayer," I replied. "What you are doing right now. Noticing. Taking it in. You are praying."

There is a bigger story. A longer trajectory. A deeper narrative that holds us. As Christians we are part of a people rooted in a tradition that extends over two thousand years, and we are shaped by those who've gone before, even as we are connected by the infinite God who holds the universe in love to all those around us and every human who has ever been or ever will be. Our story is even broader, deeper, wider: it's timeless and eternal. We live inside our experiences, but they are not our story. The psalmist encourages us to remember this and to tell the bigger story.

People love to quote Psalm 78:1–7, which tells us to remember the lessons and deeds of God and teach them to the next generation, to children yet unborn, so they can set their hope in God. The rest of Psalm 78—nearly seventy more verses past the encouraging part—gets specific and uncomfortable. It goes into great detail to tell the Israelites' story through the exodus and wilderness into the generations that follow, up to King David. And it's not too flattering. It tells the story of a people who, over and over again, doubted and turned away from God, and a God who over and over again cared for them. God provided, and they complained. God delivered them, and they chose captivity. God gave them what they asked for and more, and they chose scarcity and turned on each other. God led them, and they refused to follow.

Back and forth the psalm goes, like a boat rocking on the waves: the people complain; God gets angry and still provides. The people turn away; God gets angry and punishes them. Then God comes to God's senses and restores them again. They repent and say good things about God, but they don't mean it, and they continue tearing each other down and turning their back on God. God gets angry and calls them out, and then welcomes them back in with great compassion and provides for them once again. Over and over, the people are unfaithful. Over and over, God is faithful.

That is our story too. That is the ancient story of humankind and the ageless story of our faith, and our Scriptures don't sugarcoat it. The Bible doesn't make its protagonists shiny and perfect. It tells of their failures and their infidelity and God's consistency and salvation nevertheless and always. Telling this story is what the psalmist is suggesting we do, and with the rest of this psalm, he shows us how. Humans are unfaithful and inconsistent. God is faithful and trustworthy. God's faithfulness is the ground that holds us fast.

Our experiences and the things that have happened in our lives, in our families, in our country, in our world—they are the plot points, but they are not the story. How we tell them—to ourselves and to each other, to the next generation, and the one after that—*that* is the story. And sometimes we get the story wrong, and we need to go back and look at what happened again and tell a different story. And sometimes we think the story goes just one way, but the real story, God's story, is always bigger than our premature conclusions. And God's story—the true story—is *always* about hope and redemption.

Here is what is true: Tyrants have risen and fallen since the beginning of time. People violate each other's humanity and cause great and terrible harm. Constantly. Intentionally. And accidentally too. Terrible catastrophes occur—floods and fires, earthquakes and tsunamis, pandemics and droughts and accidents and wars. Horrible suffering is happening at any and every moment.

We are part of this story. It is our story too. We need to recognize it and own it. But it doesn't get to own us. Because there is a deeper, truer story that holds us all. And the reason we come together as church is to tell and hear that deeper, truer story. We come to be rooted and grounded in love. We come together to be called by God and sent into the world as people ready to bear the suffering without being swept up in it.

This is part of the story.
This is not the whole story.
The world belongs to God.

This refrain sustains me in times of horror; I have never not found this mantra helpful. I say it over and over again to myself when I need to face and bear awful news, when I need perspective to move forward.

The bigger story puts our smaller stories into context. The story we are living in understands that human beings are consistently unfaithful, and God is consistently faithful.

And in order to live in hope (which is always from God) and not despair (which is never from God), we need to narrate the bigger story. The story of God teaching us that we belong to God, no matter what, and we belong to each other, no matter what. And nothing we do or don't do can break that belonging. Even when we pretend it's not true, or forget it is true, or actively argue that it can't possibly be true, this remains the true story.

The love of God that has come near and claims us in love and for love and sends us out to live that love is still the most powerful and subversive thing in the universe. And no matter what, that does not change. In fact, in the face of tragedy, it is even more important to remind one another of this reality that holds us all. Because beyond our feeble human attention spans—when the alarm we raise and the energy we amp up over the current catastrophe becomes unmaintainable, when compassion fatigue sets in, or we get distracted by the next celebrity or political scandal, or the next terrible tragedy arrives, when we forget the people who right now seem the most pressing—God remains with them.

And God also remains with us in our own struggles and weakness, and doesn't say, like we sometimes do to ourselves, *Buck up! Your suffering is nothing compared to theirs!* No. God comes into *all* weakness because God comes in weakness. That is who God is and what God does. Jesus Christ is always with those who suffer, with the broken down and the locked up, the hungry and the outcast and the sick and the overlooked. In all the places we feel helpless and afraid, that is where God is and will always be. So I pray for the courage to look squarely and honestly at what is. To let in the pain. And then to name the bigger reality as well: This world belongs to God. We will claim *this* story and let it claim us. And will live in *this* story. And we'll narrate *this* story to each other to help each other remember. And we'll tell those who come after us so they can live in it too. And they can tell those who come after them, so they can set their hope on God and not forget who they are and what God does. And they too can live in the Way of God instead of the Way of Fear.

Our kids and their kids need to hear about when we messed up, when we said something that hurt someone deeply, when we didn't come through for someone, when we lied, or cheated, or turned our back on someone, or turned our back on God. They need to hear about when we gave up hope, and lost our faith, and forgot who we were and whose we were. Because the true story is about what *God* does. They need to hear about forgiveness, and redemption, and healing, and fresh starts, and new beginnings—because they need to know that who they are is not defined by their failure and unfaithfulness but by the love and faithfulness of God.

If the stories we tell are true, they will not be about good versus bad or us versus them. They will not make us look good or cover over our mistakes. And they will not hide the pain or suffering under layers of platitudes or distraction. They will be stories about God's faithfulness through our unfaithfulness. About how normal humans came alongside each other in our brokenness amid calamities and struggles, and how God worked through us to achieve remarkable things. How we were saved not through might and power, or by violent acts or vile words, but by God acting through our smallness, and sameness, and our willingness to look each other in the heart and recognize that the one I want to hate belongs to me too.

No matter what happens next or what comes after that, we follow a God of unfailing faithfulness and infinite compassion who works even in our consistent unfaithfulness and through our weakness to bring hope and life to us all. This is the true story, ancient and eternal. We are rooted in this story; we will keep telling it.

TEN

Surrendering: Being Empty

For six months doctors had brushed off Jen's concerns about a painful lump in her breast. Her backache had become so severe she could barely get out of bed. She went in for an MRI and expected to see a chiropractor. Instead, Jen was diagnosed with stage four metastatic breast cancer, which had spread to several organs and systems. At forty-one, Jen had been married to Brian for seven years, and their four-year-old, Ava, was the light of their world.

Jen was a dynamo, a force of life, always needing to know the next thing, always looking forward, always moving ahead. When Jen got sick, it took away her ability to know what was coming next. It took away her capacity to act on her ambition, to improve herself, to contribute to the world in the ways that felt meaningful and important to her. Her sickness forced her painfully, jarringly, into the moment. Jen was compelled to be absolutely, uncomfortably present—present to her body, present to her heart, present to the circumstances she could not change. She was acutely alert to what was still in her capacity to do or control. She became keenly attuned to Ava and Brian and to what each day brought, without knowing the day before, the moment before, what that would be. She was forced to live, as one of her doctors put it, "inside a two-foot square." So that is where we joined her.

The world was five months into the pandemic when Jen was diagnosed. All the things we knew how to do as a congregation to support someone in crisis were off the table in this lockdown life we were living. Visiting, sharing meals, driving to appointments, worshipping together in person—none were safe for us to do with Jen and her family. Our parish associate, Pastor Lisa, called me and said, "What if we offered to do morning and evening prayer with them over Zoom?"

Zoom was a new thing for us. We had been worshipping together via Zoom for only a few months. In a disconnected time Zoom had provided a lifeline of connection, even intimacy, to our congregation. So began our morning and evening ritual. At 8 a.m. and 7 p.m., in three different homes, we logged on and took up *Celtic Benediction* by J. Philip Newell.

Each time, we lit a candle and read the opening prayer for the day; held silence; then read the Scriptures for meditation; said a prayer of intercession, which opened up space for us to lift our own hearts to God and add in everything we needed to say; and finished with a closing blessing. The early weeks were filled with horror and incredulity, fear and pleading. As the months went on, there was hope when treatments worked and despair when they stopped working.

Every day we met. We came dressed for work meetings or doctor appointments, or in pajamas. We met sitting up or lying down, in the bedroom, in a parked car, in my basement away from my family. We kept showing up, and so did God. Ava sometimes lit the candle. She sometimes shared prayers, stroking her mama's soft, bald head, or curled into her arms. She sometimes waited impatiently in the next room for Mama and Dada to finish up.

The weeks stretched into months. The months stretched into a year, and still the days rolled on. Pastor friends were incredulous I was still doing this. If you had told me that every morning and every evening for a year and a half I would begin and end my day Zoom praying with a family going through hell, I would have said, "You have the wrong person."

But I can't put words to what the experience began to mean to me. The freedom to be with and for each other in this space was palpable. Jesus was with us. There was no pressure, only privilege. We held boundaries, honoring time off. We welcomed in visiting family or friends or those who joined from a distance. These daily prayers never became a burden; they were always a welcomed marker of time and connection. Time itself seemed suspended when we were together this way. There were days one or another of us couldn't make it; prayers carried on. They anchored us all. They drew us into something deep and sustaining, something beyond what we could have created or continued.

You and I are the very generosity of God,[1] Meister Eckhart tells us. The life of God is lived through us—the word of God that comes from God returns to God in us, through us. Jesus's dynamic belonging to God and the world is our life. We exist as the generosity of God poured out into being, into motion and light and noise.

And some part of us knows this. We know it like a longing, a recognition, the home our souls yearn for deeply, the vitality we brush up against, the vibrancy we catch glimpses of. It is realer than real; there are no words that can explain it, no way to capture the fullness and completeness of the moments we taste it. We spend our lives aching to experience it, but it can't be generated or harnessed. It can't be summoned on command or saved up for later. It can only be received. We receive this life only by letting ourselves drop into our own inability to get there.

---

1   "The Generosity of Infinite love in an act of love, creates us in the image and likeness of love for love's sake alone, moment by moment, moment by moment. The generosity of God is poured out into our life such that we are the generosity of God. Apart from and other than the generosity of God we are nothing, we are nothing, we are nothing at all." Finley, *Meister Eckhart's Living Wisdom.*

This is infuriating to us! Life is busy. And it's full and it's complicated and it's hard. We easily get caught up in the clutter, stirred up in the fervor. The noise in front of us and within us feels so loud and so urgent and so relentless. It feels *important*. It *demands* our attention. And we give it willingly. Because it feels *good* to accomplish things. It feels *good* to measure and weigh and gauge. Being able to determine that we're either *really losing ground* or *really getting somewhere* feels *good*.

But, in Psalm 62:9, the psalmist reminds us:

Those of low estate are but a breath,
    those of high estate are a delusion;
in the balances they go up;
    they are together lighter than a breath.

This may be true, but *not* comparing, *not* achieving, turning empty-handed to face the nothingness that hovers underneath all the doing, feels *terrifying*. The emotion that might overtake us! The helplessness that might engulf us! The planlessness, purposelessness, and dread of unworthiness that might swallow us whole if we stopped moving and talking! If we stopped bracing up our souls and dropped vulnerably into the nothingness!? *No, thank you. No way.*

So we settle for near misses. We settle for easy satisfaction that doesn't last. We settle for full bellies instead of full hearts, and completed to-do lists instead of the completeness of souls deeply connected to other souls. We settle for the oars of striving and the rudder of giving, instead of the helpless wave of love that might crash over us and submerge us if we were to simply receive and accept.

But sometimes the illusion of invincibility catches up with us. Sometimes we are forced into that place of nothingness. Or someone we care about is. And we have a choice to avoid or draw near.

After a few months of praying together daily, we opened up Sunday evening prayers to the whole congregation. Everyone was invited to log in on Zoom to pray with Jen for healing. Always a half dozen or so folks showed up each week to share this time with each other. Jen and Brian were open and real about what they were going through. The congregation held them with great care and deep love. Together the community bore witness to the astonishing love Jen and Brian shared, to their wrenching honesty, to their willingness to bear, and let us bear with them, fatigue and anger, sorrow and hilarity, absurdity and anguish. We came in our emptiness; we came surrendering together.

There is nowhere we can flee from God's presence. God permeates all of life. God is present in the storm. But so much of our lives are being lived through the distractions rather than living the life the distractions are distracting us from. Thanks be to God, despite all our resistance, from time to time we are plunged after all into the deep, and we experience that "without which our lives are forever incomplete."[2] And there reawakens the longing for what is most true and real.

We experience it in a tender and intimate gaze of complete acceptance, or in the heart-wrenching moment a beloved slips quietly from this life. It comes in the from-your-toes laughter that sets your very cells dancing, or in the breath-catching presence of a wild animal's quiet splendor that brings the hairs up on your arms. These moments that overtake us with the brief and overwhelming sense that we are interwoven with another, with all others, with the whole earth, the very universe, and that however terrible any one thing, or many things, might be, all is well, all is well, and all will be eternally well![3]

---

2   Finley, *Meister Eckhart's Living Wisdom*.
3   As Julian of Norwich reminds us.

The only way to this place of fullness of life coursing through us is through emptiness. It is simply to surrender. To face the nothingness. To embrace the discomfort. To both let go of our striving to get to something real and to release our fear of getting to something real. It is to cultivate what James Finley calls "a stance of least resistance"[4] to being overtaken by such encounters and experiences. In other words: we wait. We wait for God.

For God alone our souls wait. Our souls know what they are waiting for; they are just waiting for us to join the waiting. And here, in this surrender to the waiting, we and God together—in this dynamic motionlessness of waiting with each other, for the other—here is the ground of our being. In God, with God, waiting in hushed wonder together. At the deepest part of us, in the darkness way below the surface when light is off or absent, in the silence deep beneath the shallow quiet of a noiseless moment, in the bottomless stillness underneath all our movement and motionlessness, the vast emptiness—there is God. God is with us. God is closer to us than our own selves. In our absolute nothingness is God's infinite everythingness. We are the generosity of God.

One of the prayers we prayed every week with Jen included the words, "May I be well in my own soul, and part of the world's healing this day."[5] Jen began to see the struggle within her own body as a vehicle for participating in God's healing of the world. She lifted up needs of others and the pain in the world. Norm and Dennis in our congregation were diagnosed with cancer several months after Jen, and she regularly prayed for their healing while we prayed for hers.

4   Finley, *Meister Eckhart's Living Wisdom.*
5   J. Philip Newell, *Celtic Benediction: Morning and Night Prayer* (Grand Rapids: Eerdmans, 2000), 41.

Morning and evening, day after day, we logged on and lit that candle. We told God what we really most longed for, and we told God how we really felt about it all. We helped one another watch for God in the midst of all that was happening. We sat empty. We lived in the helplessness and impossibility alongside each other. When one or another of us did not have faith, did not have hope, did not have words, others of us did. When there was anger, we lifted it to God. When there was humor, we shared it generously. Tears flowed. Silence held us. Swearing and God-talk were equally welcomed. Updates on favorite TV shows, engrossing novels, and annoying errands were woven in with updates on scary scans, invasive treatments, and excruciating phone calls with doctors. Rage and recipes lived side by side in these conversations. Our ordinary, day-to-day lives were right up against horrific suffering and pain as places we watched for God together. We sought God's action and waited for God's deliverance. We cried out to God in our distress and reached out to God with our thanks.

All this time the pandemic was ongoing. Our ability to be together with Jen and her family in person was severely limited because of the risk it posed to her immune system. We had a few outdoor gatherings, but the majority of our living with and loving each other happened in these intimate daily encounters over Zoom. Except for the retreat.

Jen, Brian, and Ava were retreat lovers. The all-church Sabbath retreat was scheduled for November, and we were looking forward to it. But by the end of October the Covid numbers were bad in our area, and our session (church council) decided to postpone the retreat until May. Then we realized that it was very possible Jen would not be around for a May retreat. So we decided to go ahead with it.

The rules from Jen's oncologist were strict. We were determined to abide by them. We would all be masked the whole time. Meals would be eaten with people sitting spaced out and windows open. Brian, Ava, and Jen would use separate dishes from the rest of us. Each person attending would Covid-test twice—once several days beforehand and once the morning of departure. In the end, twenty-five or so of us were able to go.

I had thought I was in charge of the church retreat, but it turns out that everything fun and meaningful was planned by Jen. She polled every person for their favorite pop song, and our first night featured an exuberant dance party. Jen brought all the ingredients for family-friendly cocktails, and she and Brian got busy with a blender while Ava came around with preprinted menus and took everyone's order, delivering drinks to all. We kept their family tradition of coffee break at 10 a.m. with a selection of fresh pies.

The whole retreat was shaped around Psalm 62. On our last morning, Jen requested that we chant it together, like we had done weekly in worship with Psalms before the pandemic. So we joined our voices and sang,

> My soul finds rest in God alone,
>   my salvation comes from God.
> For God alone my soul waits in silence,
>   surely my hope is from God.
> God alone is our rock and our salvation, our fortress;
>   we shall never be shaken. . . .
> Trust in the Lord at all times, O people,
>   pour out your hearts before God,
> God is a refuge for us. (vv. 1, 5–8, paraphrased)

Even as her pain got worse and her energy waned, Jen was fully present to her life and let us be present with her in life. We drew near to one another, near to her suffering, near to our own nothingness and need. In our emptiness and surrender, we experienced each other as the generosity of God.

ELEVEN

Prayers for Receiving What's Difficult

PRAYER FOR THE REMEMBRANCE
OF A PAINFUL DAY

This prayer is by Jen Rainey, whose story is told in the "surrendering" and "dying" chapters of this book.[1]

Dear God,
One year ago, this day taught me the lived definition
   of horror.
It brought me to my knees. There was begging and
   pleading.
Fear, sadness, confusion, and anger
flooded in and enveloped our visions of the future.
It felt like there was no escape.
Why, God, does this type of pain exist in the world?
Why do beautiful things get ripped away or slowly,
   painfully destroyed?
Why can't I go back to what was?

---

1   Jen was a liturgy lover. The reason we had sign language in our Zoom
    worship was that Jen emailed me shortly after we moved worship
    online. "I find myself longing for interaction. Could we form a tradi-
    tion using sign language?" We added ASL for "thank you," "hooray,"
    "I see you," "I miss you," and "I love you" to help us respond to each
    other without interrupting the flow of the service.
        When we first found ourselves in pandemic lockdown, she invited
    us to share how we were experiencing God and God's provision by
    answering with a photo, "Where do you see/hear/feel/know God
    within the walls of your home right now?" She saw this as a way to
    help us both be aware of how God was meeting us and witness God's
    presence in each other's spaces. Jen's photo was a plate of chocolate
    chip cookies sitting on a table next to a candle, with the words, "I've
    unexpectedly experienced creativity, gratitude, delight, and pleasure as
    I've prepared meals this week."
        For the one-year anniversary of her cancer diagnosis, Jen wrote a
    prayer for liturgy to be shared by the community. We were not able to
    mark that day together, so I gave Jen the last word at her funeral and
    read her prayer aloud. The prayer includes Ps 139:1–6.

Breathe in the breath of the life you have now.
Let the tears of mourning cleanse your spirit
so your inner world may be gentle and blessed.
Feel the ground beneath your feet,
that same ground that you fell to on your knees and
     face,
holding you today.
Let the fears and grief arise,
and see that you are not alone—
we share this human suffering.

O LORD, you have searched me and known me!
You know when I sit down and when I rise up;
     you discern my thoughts from afar.
You search out my path and my lying down
     and are acquainted with all my ways.
Even before a word is on my tongue,
     behold, O LORD, you know it altogether.
You hem me in, behind and before,
     and lay your hand upon me.
Such knowledge is too wonderful for me;
     it is high; I cannot attain it. (Ps 139:1–6 ESV)

God, I am tired of begging you and pleading with
     you for what is good.
I am told that we are held in your love.
I breathe in one breath of rest in you.
The lightness in my chest floats out
and I feel the presence that holds us.

My broken heart beats with longing for healing;
my mind keeps me from experiencing what you've
     already bestowed upon us.
I bring my whole self, to be connected to your love,
     God.
I ask for you power to be made perfect in this
     weakness.

On this day, we remember.
We wonder what is coming.
We let go of the past.
We gather to better feel you in this moment,
to experience the ways that you were, and are,
and will be with us and for us when our worst fears
    come true.
Amen.

FOR THE DAY AFTER THE WORST DAY

*A blessing for the times death has won. A prayer for Holy
Saturday.*

"It is finished."
It simply does not get worse than yesterday.
The world has ended.
And then there was evening and there was morning.
The second day.

Today is the day after the worst day of all.
Yesterday happened.
We are stripped of illusions now.

We have stared evil in the eyes, and it has won.
It's OK to lie down and curl in on yourself for a little
    while.
It's OK not to be vigilant today.

Today is the day of not knowing and not doing.
It's OK not to know. It's OK to just be.

This is a day for silent shock and hushed sorrow.
It's a day for heaviness, and slowness,

and not talking too much, or too loudly.

This is a day to tread tenderly on the earth,
to respect the pain that each one bears,
to be gentle with yourself,
and cautious with each other.
To eat simply and sleep hungrily,
and leave the lights and your shoes off.

Between the Friday and the Sunday came
      a Sabbath day.
The greatest drama of all creation and eternity
pauses
for the day of remembering God is God,
      and we are not,
in an inconvenient,
and even ironic,
place in the story.

It stops at the absence of God from the earth;
the death of it all;
the day after the worst day.

And it stays here a bit.

Sometimes Sabbath is for keening.

After the worst day of all comes
      the day of nothing left to lose.
So rest in the gaping hole of today.
It's OK to pause here. (God did.)
It cannot swallow you whole.
It's OK to stop and not look ahead.
Yet.

THIS IS NOT THE WHOLE STORY—A LITANY IN TRAGEDY

> This is part of the story.
>> *(Pause. Take a breath. Let it in.)*
> This is not the whole story.
>> *(Pause. Take a breath. Let it in.)*
> The world belongs to God.
>> *(Pause. Take a breath. Let it in.)*
> *Repeat as needed. Let God meet you here.*

PRAYER FOR THE (UN)SUSTAINABLE—A RED SEA PRAYER

> God, the temptation is high for us to settle for
> what is.
> The routine is largely sustainable.
> The pressures are mostly manageable.
> We don't rest,
> but at least we have work.
> We are not peaceful,
> but at least we're maintaining speed.
>
> We trust in the idea of a good God who gives life.
> But when it comes to living,
> we'd rather just keep getting by
> than risk putting that trust to the test,
> if it's all the same to you.
> Because it appears that the way from sustainable slavery
> to life-giving freedom
> is through sure and certain death.
>
> God, if we're honest,
> we would rather skip that part.

If we just keep continuing what is,
maybe we can skip the hard parts.

But you want more for us than this.
And the hard parts come anyway.
So help us be still.

When the terror and the fear rise up,
help us watch for your salvation.
When the water is high, and the enemy close,
and we will surely not survive this,
help us rest in you.

You are the God of resurrection and new life.
You create, and recreate, and redeem, and deliver.

You made us for life.
We are made for connection with you and each other,
for freedom and promise,
for hope and belonging.
Be still, you say, and I will show you this is so.

And so we will stop.
We will be still.
And you will lead us from death to life.

May we come out the other side,
no longer captive,
but ready to live,
brave and connected,
fearless and whole,
with real trust in a real God,
who both delivers us from death
and gives us life.
Amen.

PRAYER TO LIVE IN THE TRUE STORY

(Pronouns can be made plural for communal prayer.)

God, please show me the stories I am telling myself
that are holding me back from the fullness of life you
    have for me.

Destroy my stories of self-protection
and make me vulnerable and open.

Heal my stories of injury
and make me a conduit of your healing.

Forgive my stories of enemies
and make me a courageous peacemaker.

Break open my stories of irreconcilability
and make me a willing listener.

Redeem my stories of wrongedness
and help me join in your ongoing justice.

Release me from my stories of grievance
and help me to grieve.

Quell my stories of despair
and teach me to hope.

Set me free
to know and share your joy,
to receive and share your love,
to bear and share your hope.
Help me to live in your true story.
Amen.

A LITANY FOR THE LIMINAL—PRAYER
FOR A NEW YEAR OR ANY TRANSITION

Standing on the threshold,
all we've left undone smirking in our periphery,
all we carry with us a finger's breath away,
    waiting, waiting.
Unfinished business clings heavy, disappointment,
pressure, expectations straining at the seams.
And what we would love to step out of
and leave behind in an unwashed heap on the floor
abandoning on tipsy tiptoe, light and free.
It's all right here, balanced, but barely,
on the threshold.

One day is pretty much the same as the last.
Let's not kid ourselves.
One day is completely new and
altogether different.
Anything can happen.
Anything.
We belong to you.
(Pause and take it in.
It's beyond taking in, really.
Just pause, then, as near the reality as you can stand
for as long as you can stand it.)
You.
Outside time, but
entering all olds and news,
permeating every yesterday
and each today, inhabiting already all
tomorrows, before they come upon us,
unannounced but right on schedule.
You. To whom
we belong.

Meet us here, Holy One, on this threshold.
Holding for us what was, carry us into what will be.
Drawing from strength we've been steadily building
throughout the years,
exhaling the rubbish we've been steadily breathing
throughout the years,
taking in instead the clean, the fresh,
timeless promises and bracing hope,
sucking them deep into our lungs,
with mouths and hearts wide, thrown open,
featherless, and trusting,
filling our strong bodies
and sturdy dreams, awakening
with gentle possibility and mighty grace, meet us on
    this threshold.

For the considerable stumbling we have ahead, grace.
For the remarkable triumphs yet to come, grace.
For the hot tears and searing pain before us, grace.
For the unrestrained laughter on the horizon,
and the astonishing joy waiting
around the corner, ready to spring, grace.

And to love.
Oh, to love.
(To You, Love, we belong, after all.)
For this we pray.
In all things. All people. However
we might, faltering and
faithful, trembling and
tenacious, may we
Love.

For this, then,
Holy Love, eternal, entered-in You,
for the new year and all it holds,

for the past however it persists,
for love brimming over and unrelenting,
and for Us
each one, standing
here on the threshold of
whatever may be,
grace.
Amen.

FOR ABSENCE—A BLESSING FOR THOSE APART

*A prayer for recognizing the absence of loved ones on a holiday,
acknowledging those who've died, or who are ill and can't be
with family, for the deployed or incarcerated, the long-distance
and the lost.*

They say, "Absence makes the heart grow fonder."
We know absence makes the heart grow poignant.
The absence of those we love and miss today
comes like a lump in the throat,
a pressure in the chest,
tears, gulped away.

Their faces rise before us,
their voices echo in the silence,
the touch of their hands brushes us in the stillness.
Longing has asked for a seat at the table of our heart
    today.

But we're tender and afraid,
and this day is for thanks, not for sadness,
so we turn away from longing,
pretend it isn't here,
and ask ourselves instead, with forced
smile, "What are you thankful for?"

batting away the hand of longing
as it reaches for our heart.

Let's not.

Today, instead,
let's welcome longing in.

Let's take its coat,
hug it tenderly,
offer it a seat,
and then feed it generously.

Given a place at the table,
longing will speak kindly to absence,
pat sorrow's shoulder,
laugh with memory,
draw out awareness,
and pull up a chair to tap the seat of honor
for gratitude.

Our hearts will be full.
And we may end up feeling, after all,
the presence of all who are not alongside us today,
here within us.

We may sense our belonging to them,
connection not only unbreakable
but strengthened this day.

Because longing,
given place and welcome,
made comfortable and free,
settles in,
makes itself at home,

and eventually reveals in us
its true and full self:
Love.

I AM REPENTING—A PRAYER WITH PSALM 46

I am repenting.
I've stopped pretending chaos isn't chaotic.
I am being honest about trouble,
and I may walk into trouble for being honest.
But here it is:
I hear the roar of the storm.
I see the shaking of the earth.
I tremble at the persistent upheaval.
I cower at the threatening turbulence.
It is tumultuous.
I feel vulnerable.
And still.
Still.
I am still.
And God is present.
Very present.
A very present help.
A very present help in trouble.
God is my refuge and my strength.
I am repenting.
In God I trust.
Amen.

A PRAYER FOR SURRENDER

O Lord, my God,
Give me courage to face the nothingness in me
and in the world.

Help me to surrender my striving for
        somethingness,
and all the tools I use to measure my worth.

Take away the things that that are killing me,
knock over the things that are propping me up,
remove all obstacles preventing me
from receiving your love and welcoming your
        grace.

Where I am lost, Lord, find me.
Shake me out of unrest
that I may return to rest.
Free from estrangement
that I may be connected once again.
Bring me back to the core of my being,
the deepest part of me that recognizes you,
and knows what it is to be me, beloved, belonging,
        and free.

Summon me back
into the hope that does not disappoint.
Immerse me in your love.
Return me to you, the Source of my life,
that I may be fully alive.
Let me be fully alive.
Amen.

GOD WITH US—A PRAYER FOR TRUST

Holy God who cannot be contained,
you make your home among us,
between us,
within us.

We are afraid.
But you are trustworthy.
Help us in our fear.

We are weary.
But you give rest.
Help us abide in you.

We are confused.
But you hold all things.
Help us in this unknown.

We are vulnerable.
But you are strong,
and you came into weakness.
Help us in our frailty.

We are lost.
But you are the way through.
Help us trust in you.

Give us peace now as we sleep.
Hold us in the love of Jesus Christ,
now and forever.
Amen.

A PRAYER FOR REST IN TIMES OF UNKNOWN

God, this life is strange.
I'm weary and afraid; I'm bored and confused.
I want to live into the future,
but don't know what that future is yet.

We miss each other, O Lord;
I miss the ones I love.

My imagination is limited.
I can't picture what you might do.
But these things are true, whether I feel them or not,
    believe them or not:
No death, no matter how big or small,
gets to define who we are and where all this is going.
In Christ Jesus, we are forgiven, connected, and made
    whole.
The earth and everything in it—
this whole story from beginning to end—
belongs to God.[2]

So I will rest.
I will trust you with my life.
I will entrust to you all those I love.
In sleep, feed and grow my imagination,
so I awaken more to hope tomorrow.
Fill me with love,
so I awaken to our hope in you.
Amen.

---

2 These words were used in worship as our Assurance of Grace after the
Prayer of Confession throughout the whole Covid-19 pandemic.

TWELVE

Practices for Receiving What's Difficult

THIS IS THE STORY—A JOURNALING PRAYER

List observations about the painful or difficult situation you are encountering.

> Describe it. Use your senses. Explain its current impact on you or on the world. What are you feeling? What needs are unmet? Don't hold back. Write until you have finished expressing it all.

Then draw a line under what you have written.

In all-caps write,

> THIS IS PART OF THE STORY.
> THIS IS NOT THE WHOLE STORY.
> THE WORLD BELONGS TO GOD.

Then draw another line under that and begin to write.

> Where have you felt held in the midst of this? Who has seen you? Where is care happening? Compassion expressed? What beauty do you notice? Glimpses of hope? What words, tastes, or signs of promise or love or healing have you heard or felt?

> What else is going on at the moment—in your family, in the community, in the world? (Perhaps stop and sit at a window for a few minutes and make some observations about the sky or activity around you.)

When you are finished, offer the experience to God in prayer.

HELLO! MY NAME IS . . . : A JOURNALING EXERCISE OF REPENTANCE

Repentance is exchanging our way of seeing things for God's way of seeing things. This change in perspective can apply to ourselves as much as to anything else. There is a worship song by D. J. Butler, performed by Eden's

Bridge, called "I Will Change Your Name." The song lists labels we put on ourselves, like *wounded, lonely,* and so forth, and says that now God calls us by a new name, using words like *confidence* and *friend of God.* This is a journaling exercise of trading the way we see ourselves for God's way of seeing us. Listening to the song "I Will Change Your Name" is a nice accompaniment to this exercise.

Draw a vertical line down the middle of a piece of paper.

What do you call yourself?
What stories do you tell about yourself? These can be "bad" or "good" (e.g., "ugly," "smart," and the like). On the left side of the page, write names you call yourself that give you your identity.

Hold those names before God and ask God to show you how God sees you.
Who does God know you to be? Sit in silence a bit.

What does God call you?
On the right side, write down what God calls you.
God most often talks to us through other people. If you can't fill this side out, bring it to someone else you trust. Ask them to listen to God with you and write down what God calls you.

REPENT—A WALKING PRAYER

"To repent" means "to turn from" or "to change your mind after being with"—in other words, to exchange one way of seeing things for another. Repenting sets down the unhelpful and destructive ways we see and behave in the world and picks up, on purpose, Jesus's way of trust in

God and living in complete belonging to God and each other.

Reflect on these questions.
> *WHAT WOULD YOU LIKE TO TURN FROM?*
>> Anger? A habit that keeps you trapped? An unhelpful way of relating with someone?
>
> *WHAT WOULD YOU LIKE TO TURN TOWARD?*
>> Hope? Patience? A relationship that is supportive? A way to help someone else?

As you walk, pause at each bend of the labyrinth as you prepare to turn, or if outdoors, at every fifth step, pause and turn slightly or completely around, so you feel the sense of turning in your body.

Ask yourself, "What am I turning from?" or "What am I turning toward?" and see what arises in you.

OR

Name a different thing you want to turn from or toward at each turn. (For example, *I turn from despair. I turn toward hope. I turn from jealousy. I turn toward generosity.*)

OR

Simply say the same thing each time you turn, such as, "I turn away from fear; I turn toward Christ."

REPENTANCE IN PRAYING FOR OTHERS

Instead of being led by fear, we can be led by love, trusting that God cares more than we do about those we are worried for. And God wants to hear our worry and sadness; there is nothing we can't say to God.

Light a candle to lift up to God someone you are worried about and entrust them, and yourself, into God's care. As you pray for this person, repent; that is, ask God to exchange your way of seeing them for God's way of seeing them.

REPENTANCE IN PRAYING FOR THE WORLD

May be done with paper as a journaling exercise.

Enemies. Allies. Poverty. Terrorists. Relatives. Vacation spot. Disease-ridden. Scary. Beautiful. We have stereotypes and prejudices about the world. These keep us from seeing clearly. But this is God's world. God loves this world and everyone in it. God does not totalize people like we do. God is always opening us wider to God and each other, connecting us more deeply to God's love.

As you pray for the world, name the stereotypes you have. Select a place, and acknowledge your stereotypes about that place and those who live there.

Then replace those labels in your mind with "Beloved." If you are doing this with paper, write down the stereotypes first. Then, as you pray, cross them off and replace each one with the word *Beloved*. If you are doing this with candles, say "Beloved" as you light a candle for each place and the people who live there. If using a map, write the word *Beloved* on a scrap of paper and place it with your candle on the places and people you are praying for.

Entrust the people in each place to God. Invite God to show you how God sees them.

GREETING IMPOSSIBILITY—A WALKING PRAYER OF SURRENDER

Walking In

> Imagine you are walking into the center of yourself, past all the layers, defenses, and barriers. Right to the tender, vulnerable, true you.

The Center

> Let yourself stay there a bit. Greet your own impossibility. Feel the emptiness. Sit a minute with your own experiences of nothingness—those from this past week or this current chapter in your life. Name them. Where does your weakness rise up? Where do you feel helpless or afraid or lost? Stay with them, make room for them. They cannot destroy you.
>
> Let God meet you right here. At your very center is where God's love is already waiting for you.

Walking Out

> From death to life, from despair to hope, God's resurrection enables us to live free and to love bravely.
>
> Can you sense God's love holding you as you return through the layers, twists, and turns to reemerge on the surface?

GOD IS MY HELP—A WALKING PRAYER

"God is our refuge and strength, a very present help in trouble" (Ps 46:1).

God is not a helper, looking at our trouble with us. God is Help itself. Our refuge in the midst of trouble.

Walking In
    As you wind around the path, imagine yourself walk-
    ing through the trouble in your life.
        Quietly or silently, name to God the tumult and
        trouble, and expound on what is troubling about
        them. Pour them out to God uncensored.

The Center
    When you arrive at the center, imagine arriving into
        God's presence. Arriving at help. Refuge. Strength.
    Sit or stand; stay as long as you wish.

Walking Out
    When you're ready, walk back through your same trou-
    bles and pay attention to what you feel and sense.

PART THREE

Receiving What God Is Doing

THIRTEEN

Participating: Being What God Is Doing

Our neighborhood has an idyllic scene every morning and afternoon. In the morning—part of the year, before the sun is even up—streams of children, parents, dogs, and strollers flow through the streets to converge on one central, busy thoroughfare where this body of humanity and chatter pours down the hill to the elementary school to pool up in the school yard and wait for the morning bell. Fifth-grade crossing guards with their blazing vests and giant orange flags direct the vehicle and human traffic, and the whole thing gets repeated in reverse back up the hill in the afternoon.

Our own tributary joins up to this river just up the street from our house. Beginning in kindergarten, my children and I walked to school and home, often with our dog, and for those first few years, depending on the time of year, with little sister in a wagon, stroller, or sled with a giant bike flag merrily bobbing off the back of it.

In second grade, the family milestone was that the kids could walk by themselves, which they were quite proud of. (One day early in second grade, Maisy came through the front door in desperate tears because another mother had seen her walking alone and had insisted that a crossing guard accompany her to her block. I had to phone this good Samaritan and inform her that Maisy was not in need of rescue but was exercising her newfound independence.)

Owen was accustomed to walking to and from school when one day I was going to be away, and Andy would be in the middle of teaching at Luther Seminary. Neither of us would be home to receive him. So we decided that second-grader Owen should walk all the way to Daddy's office and meet him there. Luther was another four blocks or so up the hill from the turnoff to our house. Owen had been there, certainly, but not frequently, and never had he gotten there by himself.

He was nervous. We drew him a map and put it in his backpack. I emailed his teacher to let her know what Owen would be doing that day. I contacted a friend—a pastor at the church right on the banks of this twice-daily river of children—to ask him to keep an eye out for Owen as he passed by that afternoon.

Owen's best friend's mom knew of this plan, as her son and Owen would normally walk together as far as our street. Unbeknownst to Owen, she told a few other moms, who were embedded in the flow of humans, dogs, and strollers or who stationed themselves at various street corners along his route. When the bell rang that afternoon, Owen's teacher checked in with him to be sure he knew his plan.

Owen pulled out his map, bolstered his courage, and set off—a tiny boy on his solo journey. But as he progressed up the hill, the text messages started coming into my phone. "He's just passed me at Hillside!"

"Owen spotted crossing Buford. He is so focused and intent!"

"He's doing great! Just made it past Speedy Market!"

On he marched, bravely up the hill, in the world "alone," nervous, and excited. All the while, he was oblivious to the web of support that held him. All the while, people all around him were watching and silently cheering him forward. Imagining the joy of all these scheming people surrounding my unsuspecting son on his brave journey made me laugh out loud (and maybe cry a little).

There's a phrase that we hear every year in the Christmas story that has gotten lost in translation. It's when the choir of angels sing, "Glory to God . . . and on earth, peace among those whom he favors" (Luke 2:14 NRSV). It's also been said, "Peace on earth to men of good will" (NIV), or "Peace on earth to those with whom God is pleased" (NLT), or "Peace to those on whom his favor rests" (NABRE).

This doesn't actually mean God is giving peace to just a few good folks whom God especially loves more than everyone else. The Greek word here, translated as "favors," means "delighted by, pleased in." It's the same word God speaks over Jesus at his baptism; *This is my beloved child, in whom I am deeply pleased*, in whom I delight!

So when those ecstatic angels who cannot contain themselves blast their joy into the faces of the stunned shepherds, what they are singing is, "Glory to God in the highest heavens! And on earth, peace among humans, in whom God utterly delights!" What they are saying is, "Y'all humans are God's favorite! God is magnificent, and endless belonging flows among God's very own beloved children!"

"Woohoo! God is coming in to share life with the delightful humans!" the angels proclaim. "And you—ordinary shepherds, doing your thing, looking after your sheep here, minding your own business, thinking you're out here in the night all alone—are part of this story! Beloved, wonderful humans! God is coming to participate in life with you, so come participate in this moment of God's arrival!"

God has come for whole world. Every person here belongs to God and to the rest of us, and the whole wide thing of it fills God with joy. Our ordinary lives participate in this tapestry of care, this web of connection, and none of it is absent the presence of God. And for most of it, that presence of God comes through one another.

All these years later when I think back to that day, I see the whole neighborhood from a bird's-eye view. Owen's little journey up the street, surrounded by all the attentive observers and silent cheerers who claimed him as their own, who rooted for him and looked out for him. With only a pause to consider the scene from above, that moment unfolding on the ground below floods me with love. I feel rising pressure in my chest and welling tears in my eyes, love for all humankind. For each little person participating, doing their thing, and all the little people watching out for each other and rooting for each other along the way.

In every place, and every time, at every moment, scenes like this are unfolding. Ordinary scenes of humans humaning, lives participating, God delighting. Imagine the angels' perspective and God's affectionate view of us living our everyday bravery and belonging, participating in the shared dance of life, often without even being aware that's what we're doing. It's utterly enchanting to contemplate.

Each life gets to be part of glory to God and peace on earth and goodwill among all beloved human beings on this whole wide earth. Each life participates. We are all in this giant web of support with and for each other, even when we think we're alone. And each of us fills God's heart with delight. All of us together? Living that connection? It's magical. And when we look out for one another, we are what God is doing in the world.

FOURTEEN

Noticing: Attuning to What God Is Doing

W hen my daughter was little, she couldn't wait to go to school like her big brother. She asked her preschool teachers for homework. She taught math in the living room to a rapt assembly of attentive stuffed animals. The summer before kindergarten, she told every grocery clerk and coffee-shop barista that she would be starting kindergarten soon. She laid out her first-day-of-school outfit in July. *This kid is ready!* we thought.

On the first day of kindergarten Maisy excitedly got dressed, put on her backpack, and rushed eagerly down the sidewalk to the elementary school building, where she had dropped off and picked up her big brother so often. Only this time, she would get to go inside and be a student herself. Her anticipation was electric.

We arrived at the classroom, filled with parents and kids, hanging up backpacks, finding name tags on the tables. It was loud and busy, swirling with anxious energy. Maisy took one step inside the door and stopped dead. Her body tensed like a tiny statue. Then she burst into wild tears. "No, no, no. Mama! No! Don't go! I can't do it. No, Mama!"

The other parents looked on with open sympathy and barely disguised relief that their own kid wasn't in such a worked-up state.

I took Maisy into the hallway and knelt and hugged her. I said everything I could think of to cheer her up. *You will make good friends! You will have fun! You have wanted this for so long, and now it's here! It's going to be OK. Your teacher is so nice.* Nothing worked.

Finally, in a moment of desperation I took a deep breath and, wiping the tears off her soft cheeks, I looked right into her terrified eyes and said, with as much confidence and certainty as I could muster, "Maisy, guess what? God has a surprise for you today. A special surprise, just for you. When I pick you up, I want you to tell me what it was."

Her sobs stopped and her eyes widened. Through stuttered breaths and sniffles she said, "Really?"

"Yes. Really," I answered. "I can't wait to hear what the surprise is when I pick you up this afternoon." She nodded and took a deep breath. I guided her gently and firmly back to her classroom door and hugged her goodbye, and she walked into kindergarten.

I rushed for the front door, my chest constricted and the tears threatening to spill out of me. When I reached the sidewalk I said aloud, "OK, God. You had better come through for her. I just told her you would, so please, please show up for her today."

The rest of the day I worried and wondered how she was doing. When pickup time finally arrived, I hurried down the hill to the school and waited with the other parents for the bell to ring. The kindergartners streamed out first, wearing ridiculous green paper hats shaped like frogs, with long, pink curling tongues bouncing off their foreheads.

Maisy spotted me and came running over, frog tongue bobbing. Her face was lit up like the sun. She started shouting before she reached my arms, "Mommy! You were right! God *did* have a surprise for me today!" I was so grateful that I can't even remember now what that first surprise was. And that day began a pattern for us.

For the rest of the week, when I dropped her off, I would tell her, "God has a surprise for you today." And then I'd beg God to give her one again. Then, when I picked her up, she would tell me what the surprise had been. A new friend in reading group. A worm on the playground. A shared lunch dessert. A silly song that made the whole class laugh.

How will God surprise you today? became a staple for her, and she'd bring it up unprompted. By the middle of the school year, it was Maisy's practice to bounce up to me at the end of the day and say, "Mommy, guess what my surprise was today?"

Finally, I began to comprehend that rather than being a risky send-off, this was a foolproof thing to say to her. That, actually, God *always* has a surprise for us. This is never not true. I eventually even made it into a mosaic and put it by our front door, *How will God surprise you today?* What I hadn't realized at first was that what God was giving Maisy—what we were calling "surprises"—was actually daily bread.

Give us this day, our daily bread, we pray.

Jesus teaches us to pray (Matt 6:7–13; Luke 11:1–13) by first telling us that this loving parent we come to in prayer already knows what we need. Prayer is not a game, not a business negotiation. We don't pray by heaping up empty phrases and platitudes, trying to get God to give us what we want, like I did to Maisy to try to get her to buck up and head into kindergarten. We begin in our place of need, like Maisy did when she asked me for help.

When I told Maisy to watch for God's surprise, it did not come from any great faith or trust on my part. I was desperate. I'd been meeting her with chipper clichés, trying to get her to dig deep within herself, muster strength, and overcome her fear. And I'd been digging deep within myself, trying to say just the right thing to make her strong and resilient. But all my efforts to get her to think differently failed. We can't save ourselves. Or each other.

It wasn't until I had nothing left to offer that I saw her in her need and recognized my own helplessness, our joint inability to overcome it. Then I was open to receiving God's provision. We needed God to meet us here. And once I acknowledged that, Maisy finally felt seen and heard by me: *This is hard. God sees your need. You are not alone. God is with you today.* Only then was she able to receive. And God gave us our first serving of daily bread, the words she needed to hear in that moment. "God has a surprise for you today."

To watch for the God who comes into our need, we must be attuned to our own and the world's needs. We are all fundamentally in need of daily bread. God meets us with just what we need for today. And we start all over the next day, asking again, *Give us today our daily bread.* To the Israelites wandering in the wilderness, God says, "I am going to rain bread from heaven for you, and each day the people shall go out and gather enough for that day" (Exod 16:4). And just like the manna, we can't get our daily bread ahead of time or save it up for tomorrow. We can only receive God's provision when it comes. Manna—which means literally in Hebrew "what is it?"—arrives when we need it, and just for today.

Perhaps our daily bread comes as such a surprise because we don't actually trust it will come. Or we don't actually believe God will give it. Or maybe it's a surprise because it doesn't come from us. Everything else we get to pretend we make happen. We can't make manna happen. God does it. For us and through us.

Faith itself is manna. We can't bank it. We are given enough for today.

This is not good news for modern, upwardly mobile people. We want control (not just of situations but of how we look navigating them). We want to store away the manna, have our spiritual pantries loaded with Costco-sized stockpiles of trust, even certainty. We want some extra mental health piled neatly on the shelf, saved up and ready for when we need it. We'd like to have our finances buttoned up tight and our long-term plans locked down. We want iron-clad guarantees of dependable relationships and assured longevity. And we think we should get what we want.

But instead, God gives us for this day what we need today, what we never could manifest ourselves. Because, of course, what we are given is Jesus Christ himself. We are given Christ's presence in our need, often through the most ordinary experiences of connection, beauty, and belonging. Jesus meets us in a kind word, a listening ear, sunshine on our face, laughter when it's most needed, being pulled out of ourselves to encounter another in *their* need. "I am the bread of life," Jesus says (John 6:35). When we watch for God's surprises, we are actually watching for the very presence of Jesus coming to us, being with us, meeting us in our need. Whether we recognize Jesus or not, he is our daily bread. God's surprise for us is always Christ.

After a while, another question joined *How will God surprise me today?* in our daily repertoire. *Who will you see today who needs kindness?* Now we were paying attention to not just our belonging to God but also our belonging to all others. The point was not "Go be kind to people." It was learning a noticing that looks beyond ourselves, a kind of attentiveness that can be uncomfortable because it attunes us to others' needs.

Most of the time, reflecting back, we recognized after the fact that someone had been lonely or sad, but we hadn't really seen them in the moment, or we had noticed them, but we'd been too uncomfortable to reach out. Sometimes we realized that someone we had shared a conversation with, laughed with, sat with, or walked home next to may have been a person that needed kindness, and without even trying to we *had* shared kindness or love. We were maybe God's surprise to *them*. We had no idea in the moment that we were daily bread, broken and shared, Jesus Christ given to them, living in and through us.

One day, Maisy, who had recently compiled a list of her favorite pop songs onto a mix CD, looked up from dunking her after-school pile of graham crackers into milk to announce, "Mom, today I saw someone who needed kindness."

"You did?"

"Yes. Devon. She was all alone on the playground, and nobody was playing with her. So I went right up to her and I sang." Throwing her arms wide, she belted out, "'I want to see you be brave!'"

"Wow," I said, struggling to keep my composure. "Maisy?"

"What, Mom?"

"Is that what you really said to Devon? Or is that what you *wish* you had said?"

She paused, then sighed. "It's what I wish I had said."

Maisy had noticed Devon in her need and let herself be prompted toward her. And while she stopped short of a full-on musical movie moment, God did give Maisy big enough brave to reach out in shared humanity to another person. She participated in the kingdom of God; she was daily bread, given for another.

We are all connected. Maisy had recognized she was part of something bigger than herself, that she belonged to something greater, and in that economy, Devon belonged to her. This is how God builds community.

After Jesus is executed, two of his followers are walking on the road to Emmaus (Luke 24:13–35), bereft and shaken. Everything they have trusted is lost. And in their utter barrenness and hopelessness, Jesus joins them as a fellow traveler. He walks with them, talks with them, listens to them. They invite him to stay with them, and all the while they do not realize it is Jesus right there alongside them, the bread of life, manna provided by God. They invite him to stay with them, and then, after he breaks bread and gives it to them, their eyes are opened. Then he vanishes. Turning to each other in wonder and clarity, they say, in retrospect, "Friends, were not our hearts burning within us?"

Jesus is with us. I want to see Jesus, and know Jesus, and recognize Jesus, and be a little bit brave about bringing it up. I want people I can turn to and say, "Did you see that?"

"Did *you* hear that too?"

"Something was happening there, right?"

"I felt it. Did you feel it?"

"Were not our hearts burning within us?"

I want people I can run home to and say, "You'll never guess how God surprised me today!" and barely get the story out before they are telling me their own tales of wonder and hope and daily bread.

This is church, by the way, as it has always been: regular people getting together and telling stories about Jesus, eating bread together, and receiving Christ there. Watching together for Jesus in the world around us. Listening for the Holy Spirit moving within us. Obeying the call of the Divine prompting us toward others and receiving Christ there. Attuning to our own and the world's needs. Giving thanks for our daily bread—Christ with us. Learning to pay attention to all the ordinary, miraculous ways we experience God's kingdom coming to us on earth, as it is heaven.

We are given faith enough for the day we are in. Each day. Faith to act or wait, to speak or be silent, to rest, and listen, and mourn, and celebrate. Faith to trust and to entrust each other to God. We are given friendship and hope, concrete ways to give and receive support, opportunities to learn and grow, and occasions to be love in action.

In our need, God provides. We are fed with the bread of life, and God makes us bread for one another, broken and given, the lovingkindness of God poured out, the presence of Christ made tangible in you and me.

But it can't be saved up. We must begin in our need, in the world's need, and watch for Christ to meet us there.

How will God surprise you today?

Who will you see today who needs kindness?

As my kids grew older, the immediacy of asking these questions daily dissipated, but they melded into our existence in a deeper way and emerge from time to time to guide us. On life thresholds or in moments of change—like heading off to camp, starting a job, or beginning a new school year—I will murmur the message in a hug or write the message in a note, "God has a surprise for you today. Watch for it." Occasionally one or another of us will spontaneously report how God surprised us or someone we saw who needed kindness that day. We are learning to pay attention. We are practicing noticing.

The world is God's, and no matter what might threaten us, God will act to bring life. We can learn to trust that the manna will come and practice receiving the bread of life. God is real today. Jesus is with us today. We will be cared for today. We will be given to others today. God has surprises for us today. This is never not true. And we will continue to watch for them and tell each other about them.

FIFTEEN

Blessing: Celebrating
What God Is Doing

"In our society, so full of curses, we must fill each place
we enter with our blessings," says Henri Nouwen. "We
forget so quickly that we are God's beloved children and
allow the many curses of our world to darken our hearts.
Therefore, we have to be reminded of our belovedness and
remind others of theirs. Whether the blessing is given in
words or with gestures, in a solemn or an informal way, our
lives need to be blessed lives."[1]

Unless we're referring to swearing, we don't think of
cursing as something we do these days. Most people don't
go around invoking supernatural downfall on others.
Except that maybe we do. We're not medieval about it.
But perhaps we have allowed cursing to creep into our
daily living and relating. Maybe we've become so fluent
at wishing harm or injury on people and things that we
don't need some special incantation to curse; we just walk
around damning people and things without even realizing
it. Perhaps we are actually more practiced at cursing than
blessing.

In Matthew 22:15–22, we encounter Jesus camped
out in the temple, fielding questions from various people,
both genuine and smarmy, those curious and wondering,

----

1   Henri Nouwen, *Bread for the Journey: A Daybook of Wisdom and Faith*
     (New York: HarperOne, 1996), September 7.

and those playing "stump the rabbi." Two opposing groups, Pharisees and Herodians, no fans of each other by any stretch of the imagination but allied in their mutual contempt for Jesus, have dreamed up between themselves the perfect question to entrap Jesus by his own words. They'd offer up a lose-lose scenario, a question with two possible answers, neither one good. There would be no way for Jesus to answer without pissing off some people or getting into trouble with others. Jesus would be trapped. It would be delicious.

So they start by pouring on the compliments. "Jesus, you are so sincere, and so truthful, and you treat everyone the same, so how would you advise us in this difficult question?"

And then, faces falsely earnest, they pop their prepared question: "Is it lawful to pay taxes to the emperor, or not?"

"But Jesus, aware of their malice" (v. 18), seeing their "desire to cause pain, injury or distress,"[2] refuses to play along. In the Greek, *evil* and *malice* are same word. "Lead us not into temptation," the Lord's Prayer says, "but deliver us from evil" (see Matt 6:9–13; Luke 11:1–4). Set us free from the desire to cause pain, injury, or distress to another. We pray this every week. *Deliver us, Lord, from malice.* Release us from the temptation to curse one another.

Jesus calls out his interrogators. "Why are you testing me, you hypocrites? Show me the coin you use to pay taxes." And so, right there in the temple, where they are not supposed to have or use money from the empire but only temple coins, they rush to pull out the coin stamped with the image of the emperor Tiberius and the words "son of the divine Augustus," in other words, "Son of God." And they show it to Jesus. "Whose image is shown there?" he asks them. "That's who this belongs to. Give to the emperor

---

2   *Merriam-Webster Dictionary,* s.v. "malice."

the things that are the emperor's; give to God the things that are God's."

The image of the empire is stamped on nearly everything we touch and do. It looks like credentials, status, salaries and titles, insurance, ranking and reputation, grades and credit scores, how much we have, how we look, what we achieve, and the labels we put on ourselves that indicate whose side we are on. We live as though everything belongs to the empire—and indeed, there is no way to escape it.

We ourselves are part of the empire; even in the temple Jesus's questioners could readily pull out the coin with the emperor's face on it, a symbol claiming who is really god. We too are at the ready—to defend ourselves, to advance ourselves, to rank and compare ourselves, to take on the role of God ourselves, or to hand it over to some voice or authority around us. Even if we don't like it, even as we disagree with big parts of it, we function pretty comfortably within the empire. And we are invested deeply in the empire succeeding. Indeed, when the structures that uphold our systems are wobbling and the empire appears to be falling apart, it is not hard to feel like the world is ending. Especially when the Christians around us seem to feel the world is ending too. We too have brought the empire into the temple.

But I keep coming back to the religious leaders'—and our, and my—malice . . . the desire to cause someone else pain. I keep returning to their hope to entrap, their willingness to destroy themselves with their own words and to wish ill on another person, taking pleasure in their demise. I'm not going to lie—I can muster me some malice. What makes this temptation so great for us that we are guided to pray against it every time we say the Lord's Prayer? What makes cursing, instead of blessing, our natural language?

I think it's that we forget that we do not actually belong to the empire. We are so often locked in the mindset of the Way of Fear, where our worth is earned and can be taken from us, where our security is up to us, where some must lose so others can win. The Pharisees and Herodians believe that discrediting Jesus somehow makes them more secure. In the Way of Fear there is not enough respect for everyone, only enough security and well-being for some. We become convinced that we must strive and compete for the upholding of our humanity. We mostly live in fear of loss, so we turn on each other, and cursing becomes the instinctive language of self-preservation. When we give over to the empire our well-being, our inner peace, our trust for salvation, or our expectation of justice or mercy or hope, we are giving to the empire what is God's.

"Whose image is stamped on this?" Jesus asks, holding the coin out to them. "That is who it belongs to." We are not stamped with the image of the empire. The empire does not own us. We are made in the image of God. God's image is stamped on us at our birth, poured over us at our baptism, traced on our foreheads from time to time in oil or ash. We are all children of God; we belong to God. We are formed in the image of Love Incarnate, God beyond limits and boundaries of nation and need, even time and space, who has given humankind to each other to care for one another, with the mandate to care for and bless the earth and all its creatures.

This is God's world. Every mountain and river and ocean and desert and creature of it belongs to God. We are God's children. Every single human being is precious and valuable to God. Jesus says, "Give . . . to God the things that are God's." That's *everything*, friends; that's *everyone*. We give each other to God; we give ourselves to God.

So we pay our taxes, we vote, we get grades and pass tests, we use insurance and build retirement funds, and maybe fill our homes with nice things, and dress for success. We pick the things we support and the things we oppose. We contribute to what we think is good and reject what we think is evil. We work together for the common good. We make our way in this world trying to shape a good life for ourselves and those who come after us by using the tools of this economy in the systems, structures, and institutions we live in, with the good and bad all mixed up and impossible to separate. Life is messy, and it's hard. We've got the emperor's image in our pockets all the time. But at the same time, our citizenship is in a deeper kingdom. We belong to a greater reality. So we pray, "Thy Kingdom come, thy will be done, on earth as it is in heaven." And we pray, "Lead us not into temptation, but deliver us from malice."

We're complicit in the empire; Lord, forgive us. Free us from the temptation of fear, the habit of comparing, and the practice of cursing. Free us to live as Christ is accused of living—with sincerity, trusting in the Way of God, speaking truth, and regarding all people without partiality, praying for the welfare of all. May we look at others, Lord, and see your image. May we give to you what is yours.

This act of giving to God what is God's—acknowledging what is God's—is called *blessing*. Blessing comes to us first from God, as an event in history. We are blessed by God, claimed by God, named by God, and so we participate in the work of God by blessing, naming, and claiming for God all that is God's. Blessing is the opposite of cursing, which falsely declares that something, or someone, is separated from God. Blessing pronounces that everything comes from God and belongs to God. This thing or person exists in God's world and is part of the whole that God has put together. And blessing sees a thing as it is, in its fullness, the darkness and the light of it, embraces it and speaks over it the good intentions of a loving God.

We can bless anything and everything. We can walk through the world recognizing the hand of the Creator in each minute detail of the natural world. But most of all, we can bless one another, recognizing the image of God in each other. No matter who the person is, we may say of the other, "Here is a blessed child of God."

We bless our beloved and our enemies, those we adore and seek with all our heart to protect from pain, and those we're tempted to hold with malice and wish ill upon.

"This one is yours, God," we say. "I give them to you. I release them to you."

"They are yours to do with as you will, to call into deeper belonging, fuller life, and truer love."

"They are yours to hold in tender care, holy wisdom, unfailing connection."

"I am yours, God; thank you for my life. Do with me what you will."

When we pray for others, naming to God their joys and suffering, we are giving to God what is God's. When we pray for our nation and the world, we are giving to God what is God's. When we pause to acknowledge the colors of tonight's sunset, notice a chipmunk in its backyard busyness, admire a bird in flight, or delight in a child laughing, when we take in beauty, or observe with tenderness our grumpy neighbor or difficult coworker, we are giving to God what is God's, and we are celebrating what God is doing in the world through this person, this thing, this moment.

Blessing holds a thing up to God's care, and it exhorts it to be even more fully itself, to live as it was created to live. *Hi, there, squirrel! You are beautiful in all your nose-twitching, nut-burying, tree-planting, traffic-dodging squirrely-ness! Keep on squirrelling, making more squirrels, and living out your squirrely part in this symphony of life!*

No matter how grim and entangled things appear at any given moment, we belong to God, not the empire, and we can opt out of the game. We can be freed from the malice. We can live in the empire without it being our god. We can celebrate what God is doing and exchange our cursing for blessing. God is holy. God is good. God is just. God is merciful. This world and everything and everyone in it belong to God. There is nowhere God is not present, nothing God cannot use. To be alive at all is a holy and marvelous thing. It is a particular job of humanity to acknowledge that. And it is the unique calling of human beings to join God in blessing the world.

Just after the verdict for the killing of George Floyd (two years after his murder) and as the Covid-19 pandemic continued to grip the world, the community of south Minneapolis came together for a "duck race" fundraiser. A local neighborhood association sponsored the race to help meet needs of local businesses and people affected by the pandemic. I was asked to share a prayer for healing at this event: healing for the earth, for relations between people, healing in general.

This assignment felt particularly fraught. Until the day before the duck race, former police officer Derek Chauvin's trial was still going on, and we did not know what the verdict or the mood would be on the day of the duck race. The intersection where George Floyd was killed had become a powerful center for gathering and grieving, a locus for art, music, and dialogue, day and night. The street was filled with symbols of resistance, tokens of sorrow, and even raised-bed vegetable gardens teeming with fresh food. But the wounds throughout our city had not even scabbed over. Piles of rubble still stood where stores, restaurants, and gas stations had been. Murals covered the boarded-up windows of shops along riot-torn streets. Protests were ongoing, particularly in Brooklyn Center, where Daunte Wright, another Black man, had been shot just a few days before by a police officer at a traffic stop. National Guard members were assembled and poised to jump into action if called.

The city was in mourning, exhausted, and on edge. Emotions were raw. Both the supportive connection and shared longing for a new way forward *and* the poignant pain and deep anger at the way things are were right at the surface. The nation's eyes were on us, and Minneapolis was feeling the gaze.

The coordinator of the event, a Black woman who had run the neighborhood association for years, reached out to a white Catholic man, asking whether he would lead a prayer. He, in turn, invited a Black man from his congregation and me, a white Protestant woman, to each offer a prayer, so that the time of blessing would more faithfully represent the community. I felt superfluous. Did a duck race need one prayer, let alone three? But I also felt moved by the request, and my heart was with my city, just as all our hearts were. The need for blessing felt acute. I felt tongue-tied, confused, inadequate to the task, and also humbled by it. What could we do but to give back to God what is God's?

When the day arrived, it was overcast and chilly. I did not expect many people to show up. But as we drove closer, my daughter and I were amazed by the crowds flocking through the streets to Minnehaha Creek. We found a parking place along a curb several blocks from the race's starting point. People wearing shirts emblazoned with rubber duckies stood at intersections directing traffic, while parents pushing strollers and people with bikes, or canes, or picnic baskets all made their way to the water's edge.

We arrived at the creek, utterly delighted by the sheer number of people that had gathered to watch rubber ducks float downstream. Joy was tangible. What a ridiculous, wonderful thing we were all doing! Other than a protest, this was the first mass gathering of humanity my daughter and I had been at in over a year, and it seemed the whole world had turned out just to be around other people doing something playful and silly.

The starter pistol fired. Thousands of rubber duckies were dumped from giant bins into the creek. And they were off!

Right away one pulled out in front. A small group broke away from the pack. Some got caught on branches and were freed by children with sticks or "duck trainers" in kayaks. Others found clever ways through brush or over rocks. And the ducks raced on, smiling straight ahead and floating merrily downstream while the people cheered and followed. Maisy and I laughed so hard at the whole thing that our stomachs ached.

The ducks took *forever*, meandering down the creek for easily over an hour. Conversations started up, and people drifted to food trucks or along the streambank to sit on a rock. Finally, the first duck rounded the bend toward the finish line. And the gathering mass went into a frenzy. A child started chanting, "Go, duck! Go, duck!" and the whole crowd picked up the chant. "Go, duck! Go, duck!" we all screamed together. Duck number 79 won the race! Thousands of dollars were raised to support local businesses that were damaged or struggling. And when the race was over, we gathered near the stage to hear the prizes the winning ducks' sponsors were awarded. But first, it was time to offer the blessing.

Except, the whole day had been blessing. Blessing upon blessing upon blessing. We had all blessed each other. We had received every moment as a gift. We had delighted in wonder alongside each other. We had celebrated our deeper belonging, this greater, healing connection that cannot be broken. This absurd shared act had already blessed us all, and the whole world around us was shimmering with beauty. We had all just been ridiculously, abundantly, uncontrollably blessed. And now, rather than superfluous, my act of blessing got to name aloud our experience of God's blessing. I got to acknowledge our having been met by God, to claim us all, and this moment, as a gift from God that we were pausing to receive together.

I looked out at the bright faces before me, their hearts opened up by this outlandish, nonsensical thing we'd all just done. I could feel community. I could see humanity. I let my heart well up with love for us all and gratitude for the Spirit's wily ways, and then I celebrated what God was doing and gave to God what is God's.

God, we come today weary, longing, hopeful, and
grieving.
But we keep learning the power of showing up together,
with and for each other,
and we recognize the great gift it is to be community.

God, your healing does not return things to how they
were
but moves things toward how they are meant to be.
Thank you for the ways healing comes through ordinary
people,
in everyday ways,
the flower planters and soul tenders,
the music makers and speech givers,
the heart holders and art creators,
the food growers and poem weavers,
the child raisers and story cherishers,
the learners and leaders,
the witnesses and the wise,
those who gather in the park to clean up trash and race
ducks together,
and the neighbors who neighbor each other,
every day, come what may.

May this time today remind us that
we all belong to each other, no matter what,
and we all belong to this earth that you love,
and we each have a part to play in the shared story of
life.

May our city become an epicenter of healing,
a wellspring of courage for the nation,
and a beacon of hope for the world.
And may we leave here today feeling grounded in love
and buoyed by joy.
Amen.

SIXTEEN

Prayers for Receiving What God Is Doing

PAYING ATTENTION—A CHARGE FOR ORDINARY DAYS

God has a surprise for you today.
Watch for it.
And when the day is done
I will ask you,
What was God's surprise for you?

You will see someone today
who needs kindness.
Watch for them.
And when the day is done
I will ask you,
Who did you see who needed kindness?

We will live this way,
you and I.
This is how we will live.
Reminding each other to watch,
asking each other what we saw.

We will be noticers,
you and I.
We will be noticers of God.
We will be noticers of other people.
God will surprise us,
people will need kindness,
and we will notice both.

We won't know how it will happen,
or when,
but every day it will happen.

We will keep watching

until we trust
that this is true.

And then we will watch
because it is true:
God has a surprise for you today,
every day.
You will see someone who needs kindness today,
every day.

Watching, asking, noticing, remembering,
we will live this way,
you and I.

Trusting God has a surprise for us,
trusting we will see someone who needs kindness
every single ordinary, holy day.
This is how we will live.
Amen.

A BLESSING FOR WHAT IS GOD'S

God, I am yours.
My life belongs to you, I give it back to you.
I give my life to love. I give my life to hope.
I give my life to being part of your healing and joy in
    the world.

God, *(name of loved one)* is yours.
Their life belongs to you; I give it back to you.
I give their life to love. I give their life to hope.
I give their life to being part of your healing and joy
    in the world.
(Repeat as needed with other names)

God, *(name of someone difficult for you to love)* is yours.
Their life belongs to you; I give it back to you.
I give their life to love. I give their life to hope.
I give their life to being part of your healing and joy
     in the world.
(Repeat as needed with other names)

CANNOT HIDE—A CONFESSION
BASED ON PSALM 139

(Words of the people in bold)

God, here with us now,
you know us completely. And you love us completely.
But it's hard to trust this.
So we try to be more loveable, impressive, or put
     together.
We push you away or ignore you because we think
we can keep our scariest or saddest parts hidden.
We struggle to love ourselves,
and we put on a mask for others.
But we cannot hide from you.

God, here with us now,
     we all belong to you and we all belong to each
     other. This can't be earned or lost.
But it's hard to trust this.
So we judge, and sort, and label, and dismiss.
We turn our backs on some people, and we cozy
     up to others.
We try to withhold belonging,
or make people earn it, buy it, or prove it.
But we cannot run from your presence.
God, here we are. As we are. With you here.
Amen.

THE OUR FATHER—A GUIDED PRAYER

> Our Father, who art in heaven, hallowed be thy name.
> *(Offer prayers of thanks and praise to God.)*
>
> Thy kingdom come, thy will be done, on earth as it is in heaven.
> *(Offer prayers for the world, for the church, for your life.)*
>
> Give us this day our daily bread.
> *(Offer prayers for specific needs of others and yourself.)*
>
> And forgive us our debts, as we forgive our debtors.
> *(Offer prayers for personal forgiveness and for tension in relationships.)*
>
> Lead us not into temptation, but deliver us from evil.
> *(Offer prayers for places where deliverance and freedom is needed within you, between you and others, and in the world.)*
>
> For thine is the kingdom and the power and the glory forever.
> *(Offer prayers of gratitude and praise.)*
>
> Amen.

ARRIVING HERE—A BLESSING FOR CREATIVITY AND WORSHIP

> *A group liturgy for an experience of making art together, retreating, or interactive worship. (Words of the people in bold)*
>
> When God's people gather,
> we are drawn into the life of God,

---

and the artistry of the Creator moves in us.
Breathe in.
(pause and breathe)
Receive.
We receive God's freedom and joy.
Breathe out.
(pause and breathe)
Release.
We release our anxiety and assumptions.

When God's people gather,
we are drawn into the life of God,
and the presence of Christ moves between us.
Breathe in.
(pause and breathe)
Receive.
We receive God's compassion and mutuality.
Breathe out.
(pause and breathe)
Release.
We release our cynicism and comparisons.

When God's people gather,
we are drawn into the life of God,
and the inspiration of the Holy Spirit moves through
　　us.
Breathe in.
(pause and breathe)
Receive.
We receive God's imagination and wonder.
Breathe out.
(pause and breathe)
Release.
We release our weariness and resistance.

When God's people gather,
we are drawn into the life of God.
A sacred space is opened for us here.
A generous moment is offered to us now.
The Triune Divine awaits our arrival.
We gladly join you here, O God!

FOR MOTHERS AND MOTHERING—A BLESSING FOR MOTHER'S DAY

"As a mother comforts her child, so I will comfort you."
(Isa 66:13)

Mothering is a messy, complicated business—
just like humaning,
with impossible expectations,
deep longings,
piercing pain,
and incomprehensible joy.

On Mother's Day
gratitude and sadness
intermingle—
as they do whenever we are really
paying attention.
The mothers
we wish we'd been . . .
the mothers
we wish we'd had . . .
the mothers
we wish were still with us . . .
the mothers
we never knew . . .
the "mothers"

we've had along the way
who made us who we are today . . .
the mothers
we've watched our daughters become . . .
or not . . .
All of their faces rise before us.

So we pause and
welcome them in,
whatever emotions they bring.

This I know:
pain does not disqualify
gladness.
And love and gratitude
do not dishonor grief and sorrow.
We are all in this together—
mothers, mothered, motherless—
children and siblings in the human family.

So,
to all mothers, thank you.
For all mothers, Lord, thank you.
And most of all, God, for mothering us,
thank you.

THE HEART OF A FATHER—A BLESSING FOR FATHER'S DAY

The heart of a father
who loves his children,
who pours into them wisdom and knowledge,
and teaches them skills,
and gives them experiences,
and watches them sleep in the night, their cheeks
    pressed against their pillows,

dreams flitting across their faces,
and prays
for their tender hearts,
and their wide-open futures,
and the pain that will pierce them,
and the joy that will buoy them . . .

the heart of a father
that breaks in pieces with his child's suffering,
and breaks wide open with his child's delight,
that beats in time with their steps,
and when danger threatens, ceases momentarily to
     beat altogether . . .

the heart of a father
that swells with his children's accomplishments,
and shrinks with their humiliation,
that is linked utterly to their hearts,
mysterious, holy, and maddening . . .

the heart of a father
that never before knew such worry,
or wonder,
or waiting,
that would give his beloved child the moon if he
     could,
would sacrifice his own life if it came to that,
and that sometimes
wishes only
to be left
blessedly
alone,
to catch his breath,
to regain his footing,
to place a hand on his chest

and feel the beat,
steady, confident, unwavering,
even when he is none of those
at the moment . . .

the heart of a father,
the heart that hangs onto this small person,
who is confoundingly both yours
and not yours at all,
the heart that lets go of this person,
always letting them go,
giving them what they need
in order to let them go
into the world
to make their own way,
and to come home into the safe arms of a father
when things fall apart,
to be held and comforted,
and stood up, and brushed off,
and sent out again,
taking with them his own heart . . .

this heart, God,
bless this heart today.

Today bless each one
who bears a father's heart.

Thank you for those who have fathered us,
whose hearts have shaped and strengthened ours,
who have clung to us and let us go,
who have loved and taught and prayed and steadied,
who have fought for us when we were wronged,
and fought against us when we were wrong,
those who've failed and flailed and forgiven,

sacrificed and celebrated and shown us the way.
Thank you for those who have shared
their own hearts with us in loud and quiet ways,
and have given us what we needed to share
our own hearts with the world.
Thank you, God, for fathers.

God bless and hold and
keep all fathers' hearts,
in your own heart today,
and every day.
Thank you, Abba,
for the heart of a father.
Amen.

A BLESSING FOR GIVING THANKS (OR A THANKSGIVING BLESSING)

Gratitude is a door into timelessness.
Stopping in wonder,
letting gratefulness swell in your heart,
rise in your throat,
and press against the back of your eyes
pulls you through the moment
into the deep reality.

Beyond everything else
and underneath it all,
we belong to God
and we belong to each other.

May today be filled with glimpses
that break through
noise and division,
anxiety and frustration,

distraction, blame, and fatigue,
to this fundamental truth:

These people belong to you
and you to them.
We all belong to God,
this whole wide world,
and life is a gift,
abundance beyond measure,
to be shared and received—
each breath and touch,
each laughter and tear,
each taste and texture,
drawing us in, opening us up,
to receive, respond, rejoice.

Pause there for a moment.
Read it again if it helps.

And when you forget
that you belong to God and these others,
may someone see past your defenses and bluster,
to your longing soul,
and may the Spirit gently nudge you back
to your true home,
the space you are known and loved in God.

And when it's a challenge,
may the grace of deep belonging hold you fast,
console your disappointment,
and give you a peek past their bluster
into the longing soul of another
who belongs to God and you,
even while they're forgetting it just now.

Gratitude is a door into timelessness,
pulling you through the moment
into the deep reality.
And these words, "Thank you,"
masquerading as simple, even trite,
are a mighty invocation,
a holy and powerful homecoming,
returning us to each other,
with whom we share all life and blessing,
and returning us in God,
from whom all life and blessing comes,
and to whom all life and blessing returns.

SEVENTEEN

Practices for Receiving
What God Is Doing

MEMORY PRAYERS—A JOURNALING EXERCISE

Concept created by Rev. Lisa Larges

God is in every moment, present with us in all things. God's power, which we experience as grace, is at work all around us. We can trust in that power and give thanks. We can begin recognizing God more often when we practice asking of any and every experience, *Where was God in this?* Use this simple method for writing a prayer to help pay attention to how God is at work in our world and in your life. If you enjoy writing memory prayers, keeping a memory prayer journal is a wonderful way to begin seeing patterns of God's activity in your life, to grow in your capacity to recognize God with you in all things, and to regularly practice gratitude.

Shaping a Memory Prayer

Reflect for a time on the past week. Find any moment that sticks out to you.

> It may have been a conversation, something you heard or read, a connection with someone, or something that caught your attention in the natural world.

Use these prompts to shape your prayer.

> I REMEMBER . . .
> GOD WAS . . .
> I GIVE THANKS FOR . . .

For example:

> I remember sitting with a friend in a corner of a quiet restaurant.
> GOD WAS in our conversation.
> I GIVE THANKS for friendship.

I REMEMBER a quiet morning reading the paper
   on the porch, before many people were awake.
GOD WAS present in the stillness.
I GIVE THANKS for new days.

I REMEMBER a painful argument with my brother.
GOD WAS in the space for hard truths to be spoken.
I GIVE THANKS for relationships that endure.

I REMEMBER taking off my shoes and stepping
   into the cool, wet grass after a long, hot walk.
GOD WAS slowing me down, inviting me to
   experience the moment.
I GIVE THANKS for rest, refreshment, and
   perspective.

NOTICING—PRAYER FOR THE WORLD

This prayer can be done as a meditation or a journaling exercise.
As you reflect on our world and your place in it, you may
   offer one or both of these simple prayers.

Thinking about this past week in your own life and the
   life of the world, where have you seen Jesus?
It may be a person, a news story, an act of kindness you
   witnessed or were a part of, or something else.

Thank God for these glimpses.

Thinking about your own life, and the life of our world,
   where do you long to see Jesus?
It might be in a particular place, or in a particular person,
   or in a problem our world is facing.

Tell God what is on your heart.

WRITING BLESSINGS—A JOURNALING PRAYER

In his book *99 Blessings*, Br. David Steindl-Rast illustrates the act of pronouncing blessings on things. For no other reason than that something exists, it can be blessed. He sees this as the way we take up the holy task given to us as human beings, of acknowledging that to be alive is a sacred gift we receive by giving thanks for what is. In this little book, he writes a blessing a day for ninety-nine days, without going back and editing, just letting them be what they are. Taken all together, it's a wonderful litany of paying attention to life and giving thanks.

Here are two examples:

Blessing 5
SOURCE OF ALL BLESSINGS,
you bless us with dreams—
dreams while we sleep and dreams in our most wakeful
moments.
May I be responsive to both forms of dreams
and pass these blessings on by living a life that is faithful
to their guidance.[1]

Blessing 20
SOURCE OF ALL BLESSINGS,
you bless us with kitchen noises—
with the sound of chopping carrots,
the rumbling from washing pots and pans,
the clinking of silverware, the clang of glass on glass,
the whistling of the teakettle, and all the homey rattle
and clatter produced by preparing food and washing
dishes.

....

1   David Steindl-Rast, *99 Blessings: An Invitation to Life* (New York: Image, 2013), blessing 5. Used with permission.

May I drink deeply from the blessing of being at home
that rings in these sounds
and make all whom I meet today feel a bit more at home
in the world.[2]

Write some blessings of your own

Pick three things you want to bless.
> They can be completely innocuous (silverware, showers, carpeting), things in nature (sunshine, thunderstorms, soil), or something internal or relational (laughter, tears, conversations, daydreams).

Then write some blessings of your own using this pattern.
SOURCE OF ALL BLESSINGS,
You bless us with . . .
May I . . .

GUSH OF GRATITUDE—A WALKING, SITTING, OR JOURNALING PRAYER

You can do this in the silence of your heart or spoken aloud. (If done with others, do it aloud.) Inside, outside, walking, sitting; you could also do it in the dark, after you've laid down to sleep. It's a great exercise for journaling; this is a list writer's delight. When done with kids or in a group, it's very different but just as wonderful an experience as when done alone.

This prayer is a mind-wandering, free-association, gratitude fest. No limits. It can be a powerful experience when offered alone—like taking an extra deep breath and feeling air in the bottom of your lungs, where you almost never let it reach. It's expanding and cleansing, and also rearranges

---

2   Steindl-Rast, *99 Blessings*, blessing 20. Used with permission.

your insides back to how they were meant to sit, and you'll find you rest deeper and more authentically for having given thanks.

Follow this pattern:
> Thank you, God, for . . .
>> Say the first thing that comes to mind, and then the next, and see where it takes you.
>> Whenever you reach a quiet heart, take a deep, cleansing breath in and blow it slowly out, and begin again.
>> Let the gratitude gush go as long as it can.
>> When you are finished, wait to see whether anything else comes.
> Amen.

VOWS FOR STEPPARENTS—A COVENANT BLESSING FOR EXPANDING FAMILY

After the couple makes vows to one another, the following blessing can be done with the child/ren.[3]

To the newly forming family:
> God makes you a family,
> and gives you to each other to be love and support
> your whole lives long.
> We celebrate and honor the choice and gift of
> becoming family together.

---

3   My sister got married in the middle of the pandemic. Her joyful wedding took place on a chilly March afternoon in a friend's backyard overlooking the Mississippi River. They wanted in the ceremony a way to make vows to the six children, a recognition that their family was expanding, that they were going to belong to each other in a new and sacred way. I created this simple liturgy to include children in a wedding ceremony and formally acknowledge the commitment a stepparent makes.

To the new stepparent:
> *[Name],* do you welcome the responsibility and priv-
> ilege of being parent to *[child/ren's name(s)]*, to stand
> with them in love and support in whatever life may
> bring, to always reflect to them the truth of Christ's
> love for them and their security in God's grace, as you
> raise them to honor their own and others' humanity?

Stepparent responds:
> I do.

To the parent:
> *[Name],* do you confirm the call of God to *[stepparent's
> name]* as *she/he* commits to care for your child*ren*, with
> and alongside you, sharing the responsibilities, duties,
> joys, and struggles of parenthood, guided by the love of
> God and the power of the Holy Spirit?

Parent's response:
> I do.

To the child/ren:
> *[Name(s)],* do you choose to welcome *[stepparent's name]*
> love and care, as God makes you family with each other?

Child/ren's response:
> I do.

Symbol of covenant bond
*The stepparent may give a ring, necklace, or other symbol to
the child/ren.*

The stepparent may say to each child:
> *[Name],* I give you this *[name the symbol]* as a sign of
> my love, a pledge of my faithfulness, and a symbol of
> the covenant we make this day.

VOWS FOR GODPARENTS—A COVENANT BLESSING FOR FAITH FAMILY

May be used alone or in conjunction with baptism or other liturgies. Adapt as needed for one godparent or more than two. Adapt pronouns as needed.[4]

Leader begins:

We are privileged to celebrate today that [*Godparent name(s)*] have been called to welcome and walk alongside [*Child/ren name(s)*]

We commission them to the role of godparent, recognizing that they bring their whole selves to this role. They are to share their own joys and sorrows, their strengths and weaknesses.

They are to model for [*Child/ren name(s)*] honesty with life's struggles and commitment in their own journeys as they seek to love fully, follow God, and share God's love in the world.

---

4   Normally, godparents have a verbal response in a baptism ceremony. But what if you want godparents but not baptism? Or what if the child is already baptized and the godparents come later? Or what if you want to appoint godparents at birth in a tradition that joins baptism with confession of faith as an adult or older-child ritual? There are many circumstances that call for stand-alone godparent vows. I wrote these godparent vows when the mother of a teenage girl approached me and shared that her daughter desired to acknowledge someone who had been an unofficial godmother to her throughout her life. The family and the woman wanted to make it official. We created a ceremony and declared the godmother relationship official. Then, several years later, we did a baby blessing ceremony for a family with ties to the church but who did not see themselves as religious and so would not be baptizing their children, but did want to appoint godparents. And then again, two years later, for their twins. Finally, I had the honor of making these same vows myself, for my goddaughter, Eleanor.

To the Godparent(s):

[Godparent name(s)], do you welcome the responsibility and privilege of being godparent to [*Child/ren name(s)*] to stand with *her* in love and support in whatever life may bring,
to always reflect to *her* the truth of Christ's love for her and *her* security in God's grace?

Godparent response:

I do.

To the Godparent(s):

Will you accompany [*Child/ren name(s)*] on *her* life journey, speaking the truth to *her* in love,
helping *her* to always honor *her* own and others' humanity as children of God?

Godparent response:

I will, with God's help.

To the Godparent(s):

Will you pray for [*Child/ren name(s)*] and challenge *her* to be faithful and brave, to find *her* own voice, to share *her* gifts, and to seek out and live into her calling in this life, whatever that may be?

Godparent response:

I will, with God's help.

Leader continues:

Let's pray.
All-embracing God, the hope of every generation,
we lift before you *these* godparents
pledging to stand with [*Child/ren name(s)*] throughout *her* life

---

as her friend, comfort, and support.

Complete their joy by your presence.

Give them quiet strength and patient wisdom
as they nurture [*Child/ren name(s)*] and offer the gift of
their presence in all of life's ups and downs,
as they walk alongside *her* in her journey,
with open ears and open arms.

We pray blessings on them, and deep joy in this role,
through Jesus Christ, our Lord.

Amen.

ADOPTION LITURGY

*Includes instructions for use in conjunction with child bap-
tism. Adapt italics portions for number of parents, number of
children, and child/ren's gender(s).*[5]

To the congregation:
Beloved in Christ, in adoption God makes us family. As Paul says in Romans 8, we ourselves have not

---

5   My friend Tricia adopted her child from Haiti, from an orphanage
where she volunteered once or twice a year to hold babies where there
were too few sets of arms and too many babies needing holding. When
she met her child for the first time, she held her baby in her arms and
whispered that she loved her little one and that she couldn't wait to be
this child's mom. And then she had to leave her baby and return home
to await the final legal hurdles that could take weeks. In the mean-
time, a bureaucratic move in Haiti closed adoptions, and for the next
fourteen months her child remained in the orphanage while my friend's
case stalled. She visited twice in that time for a few desperate days and
nights sitting in a rocker holding her baby in her arms, talking and
singing to her child, and then laying her child down and leaving, getting on a plane, and flying home alone. Finally, the paperwork cleared,
and Tricia flew back and was able to take her one-and-a-half-year-old
child home, and Tricia became a mother. The following adoption blessing was created to be included in the ceremony for baptism.

---

received a spirit of slavery to fall back into fear, but a
Spirit of adoption, by which we cry, "Abba, Father!"
And in Ephesians (1:5–6) we are told that God has
predestined us for adoption through Jesus Christ, and
that we are made joint heirs with Christ, who himself
was adopted into the lineage and family of David when
Joseph said yes to God's call to be the adoptive dad of
the Savior of the world.

*[If adoption blessing precedes baptism, include this
portion.*
    Today, when we baptize [*Child/ren name(s)*] into the
    family of God, may we each remember our own
    baptism, that we are all adopted into God's family
    and by God's grace made joint heirs with Christ.]

Today we join with [*Parent name(s)*] in offering heart-
felt thanks for the joyful and solemn responsibility
that is *theirs* by the coming of this child, and for God's
ever-abundant grace that pours joy and blessings into their
shared life and binds them together in God's covenant
love.

To the parent(s)
    Beloved in Christ, this child is a sign of God's love to
    you,
    and you are a sign of God's love to *her*,
    given by God and sustained by the Holy Spirit.
    This child is the heir(s) of your life
    and will carry the legacy of your faith into future
    generations.
    By the grace of God *this child is* made your *daughter*,
    and by the grace of God, you are made *her* parent(s).
    You are given to each other to share in this life,
    in all the joy and suffering it brings,
    and to meet Christ in the extraordinary

and ordinary moments together.
Thanks be to God.

[If adoption blessing precedes baptism, include this portion.
Today, you will make commitments to [*Child/ren name(s)*]. [*Child's/children's name(s)*] family and godparents will promise to stand by *her*, and this one small part of the church universal, gathered here today, will commit to fulfill the promises on behalf of the whole church
while [*child's/children's name(s)*] *is* in their care.

You will promise to raise [*child's/children's name(s)*] to know, and help *her* to embrace, the love and grace of God that claims *her* for life.
The adoption that began when God brought you and [*Child/ren name(s)*] together is blessed and completed today when we welcome *her* into the family of God,
and we embrace *her* into the covenant of God that is made over us in baptism.]

And so, as a sign of our affirmation of the calling of God in your life to be [*Parent name(s)*], and as a mark of God's blessing that we today uphold and celebrate, we anoint you.

Anointing of parent[s]
[*Parent name(s)*] child of the covenant,
you have been sealed by the Holy Spirit in baptism
and marked as Christ's own forever.
(*Anoint parent[s]*).

You have been called by God to be [*mother/father*],

nurturer, provider, boundary,
protector, and forever family of [*Child/ren name(s)*],
by the grace and goodness of God,
and in the strength given us only by the Holy
    Spirit.

(Repeat for each parent.)

Leader continues:
Let us pray.
God of heaven, Father and Mother of us all,
rest your Holy Spirit upon [*Parent name(s)*].
Uphold *her* as *she* parents [*Child/ren name(s)*]
Give [*parent's name*] the spirit of wisdom and
    understanding,
the spirit of counsel and might,
the spirit of knowledge and the fear of the Lord.
In your steady presence may *she* find joy,
in your loving care may *she* find rest,
in your faithful guidance may *she* find peace,
both now and forever.
Amen.

[*If followed by baptism, include this instruction.*
And let us now proceed with the baptism of this
covenant child, born by the providence of God
into this family that God has created.]

THE HEDGEHOG BLESSING—A BACK-TO-SCHOOL BLESSING FOR CHILDREN AND TEACHERS

*Children and teachers are gathered. A hedgehog stuffed animal
may be given to each one as this blessing is shared. (Words of*

the people in bold.) [6]

Leader begins:
"Gracious is the LORD and righteous;
our God is merciful.
The Lord protects the simple;
when I was brought low, he saved me.
Return, O my soul, to your rest,
for the LORD has dealt bountifully with you." (Ps 116:5–7)

Children and teachers,
God made the sun and the moon, the night and the day,
the oceans and the land, the sky and the animals;
God made the hedgehog and God made you.
So to send you back to school this year, we are giving you a special "Hedgehog Blessing."

---

6   The Hedgehog Blessing is a great example of the power and invitation of blessing. When my director of music and worship arts, Erin, and I set about to create a back-to-school blessing that gifted each student and teacher with a stuffed animal, hedgehogs were approximately our fifth animal of choice. As an analogy for God's love or care, we were initially hard-pressed to find a connection. But all the lions and lambs and kangaroos had slower shipping speeds, so hedgehog it was. But here's the miracle of blessing—all things are God's, and all things are related in the harmony of life. And so I discovered, with great joy, that the needs of our children and teachers and the characteristics of a hedgehog converged to provide exactly the right blessing for the particular moment. And as the school year progressed, I received texts and photos of hedgehogs in kids' backpacks, sitting by computers at homework time, or perched on science-classroom shelves, a reminder of God's love and presence with us in all things. I now believe (and have happily put this theory to the test) that it is possible to take anything in God's creation, hold it before God, and ask for the blessing it speaks to us in the moment, and we will find it.

Beloved Children of God:
   As hedgehogs roam far and wide and investigate
   the world,
   may you have room to discover and grow,
   may you be filled with curiosity and wonder,
   may your body move, your heart thrill, and your
   mind explore.
Bless them, Lord.
God, bless these beloved ones.

   As hedgehogs are the most deeply hibernating
   creature on the planet
   and have no problem curling up for a nap any-
   time throughout their waking days,
   may you take many breathers and breaks when
   you need them:
   brain breaks *and mask breaks* and friend breaks
   and screen breaks.
   And may you know when to let go and relax,
   and when you are tired, may you find deep
   rest.
Bless them, Lord.
God, bless these beloved ones.

   As hedgehogs are very vocal with their grunts
   and snuffles and squeals,
   so may you speak up and speak out.
   Share your joys and your sadnesses, your worries
   and your celebrations.
   May you make new friends and listen to their
   grunts and snuffles and squeals too,
   because we are all in this together.
Bless them, Lord.
God, bless these beloved ones.

As hedgehogs' quills offer protection but do not
sting or injure,
may your heart and mind and body be guarded
this year.
And may you work out conflict in ways that
bring peace instead of harm,
because in Jesus Christ, we all belong to each other.
Bless them, Lord.
God, bless these beloved ones.

The hedgehog was for ancient peoples a symbol
of resurrection,
or life after death, because God made the hedgehog immune to snake venom.
So, like the hedgehog, you too are protected;
mean or poisonous words cannot destroy you,
and mistakes and struggles do not define you.
Who you are in your deepest self
is already completely known and loved by God:
you are a beloved child of God; Jesus holds you secure.
Bless them, Lord.
God, bless these beloved ones.

As hedgehogs curl into a ball,
may you too let yourself feel your feelings.
If you are sad or angry, scared or worried,
God will join you there and hold you in it.
And as hedgehogs enjoy being held,
and not forced to come out of their ball
but allowed to uncurl when they are ready,
may you trust that you are held in God's love,
and it's OK to just rest there,
and not to move too quickly.
Bless them, Lord.
God, bless these beloved ones.

As hedgehogs lose their baby spines and grow
adult ones,
many of you will lose your baby teeth and grow
adult teeth,
which we will celebrate with you as milestones of
growing up.
But all of us get to let go of the ways that no
longer serve us in protecting ourselves,
and grow new, brave ways to stay both connected to God and other people
and true to ourselves.
Bless them, Lord.
God, bless these beloved ones.

God made hedgehogs with a strange ritual.
When they discover a new scent in their envi-
ronment—some kind of plant or object they
don't recognize—they will lick and bite it,
and make froth in their mouths that they paint
onto their spines with their tongues.
This is called "anointing" and helps them adapt
to their surroundings.
You have been anointed today as a beloved child
of God.
So like the hedgehogs, may that make you brave
to be in whatever places you are this year,
and may you have courage to face new and different things.
May you be resilient (which means that you get
better and better at recovering when hard things
happen),
and may you be adaptable (which means you get
good at adjusting to changes).
Bless them, Lord.
God, bless these beloved ones.

As hedgehogs are clever and resourceful, such as
knocking a grape off a vine and rolling over onto
it to stab the grape onto its quills and carry it off,
so may you find creative, joyful, and imaginative ways to navigate challenges, and to find and
hang onto the sweetness in this year to carry
with you and share with others.
Bless them, Lord.
God, bless these beloved ones.

God of the whole universe and of the hedgehog too,
bless these children and teachers with all these
    things, and in all these ways,
as they begin a new school year.
Amen.

A LITURGY FOR RECEIVING BIBLES

*If desired, the song "God, We Honor You" (by James E. Clem-
ens,* Glory to God Hymnal, *#709) may be used as a refrain.
The verses may be sung separately throughout the liturgy and
together in a round at the end. Another suitable hymn or song
may be used instead.*[7] *(Words of the people in bold)*

---

7   On a Sunday morning we lined up all the kids in our tiny congregation,
ranging from ages two to twelve, and presented them with Bibles: story
Bibles, or study Bibles, depending on their age. The kids were invited
to sit on the front pew, where they could see one another receive their
Bibles. As each child was called forward, I knelt or stood beside them,
holding their Bible, and said to them, by name, "God's Story is your
story." And the congregation responded to each child, "And your story
is our story." Two-year-old Robby watched with growing impatience
as person after person went up before him. His swinging legs began
pumping harder and harder, and he could barely sit still, he was so filled
with anticipation. Finally his turn came. I barely got his name out of my
mouth before he dropped off the pew and ran to me, tiny arms propel-
ling him forward, shouting, "God's Story is *my* story!" Amen and amen!

Introduction *(optional)*

Leader:

    The story of God is your story; it is our story, all together. The Bible is like a very special family scrapbook—with poetry and parables, memories and struggles, letters and songs. We trust God to speak to us through these words. The Holy Spirit uses these words to teach us, challenge us, and encourage us. And because the Bible shows us who Jesus is, it helps us see Jesus in our own lives and in the world around us.

    These Bibles tell us God is love, forgiveness is real, life is hard, people are always messing up and hurting each other, and God keeps on loving us. You might read the same thing at different times in your life, and God will use it to tell you what you need to hear, and it may not be the same thing as the last time you read it! That's how the Holy Spirit works. The stories of God and the people in this book, and the stories of God in each other's lives, help us to see Jesus and to notice how Jesus is always bringing love and healing, and inviting us to be part of it.

Hear these words from Scripture:

"How sweet are your words to my taste,
    sweeter than honey to my mouth!
Through your precepts I get understanding;
    therefore I hate every false way.
Your word is a lamp to my feet
    and a light to my path." (Ps 119:103–5)

Litany of Gratitude for Scripture

Children are called to gather around the Bibles, which are set on the table or altar.

The Word of God tells us who God is and what God is up to.
May these Bibles help you notice God and love God more!
(Sung response "God, We Honor You," stanza 1)

The Word of God tells us who we are and what we're invited to be up to.
May these Bibles help you join in God's love and blessing in the world!
(Sung response "God, We Honor You," stanza 2)

The Word of God reminds us that Jesus broke the powers that divide us from God and each other, and no matter what, God's love is the biggest and truest thing of all.
May these Bibles help you discover and celebrate God's love that claims you!
(Sung response "God, We Honor You," stanza 3)

Presenting the Bibles

When I call your name, please come to receive your Bible.
[*Name*], receive your Bible.
God's story is your story.
And your story is our story.
We love you, [*name*]!

After all the children have received their Bibles, offer the following.

Blessing

Beloved children of God, children of this congregation, we bless you. May your Bible open you to the word of God.

**We will read it together. We will listen together.
We will hear the stories of our faith together.
And the Holy Spirit will speak to us
through these words and through each other.
Thanks be to God! Alleluia!**
Sung response ("God, We Honor You" as a round) if desired.

A HOUSE BLESSING

*This liturgy uses oil, perhaps pouring a small amount on a
cotton ball in a dish. (Words of the whole group in bold.)*[8]

---

8   One of my favorite moments of shared blessing happened when our Pres-
     byterian Women group did a house blessing for Marge, a member who
     had moved into assisted living. Assisted-living apartments are not huge.
     We began in the living room, the whole shuffling lot of us, smooshed all
     together in her space and speaking aloud the hopes and intentions for the
     room. People began tentatively, "This room has such lovely light! Look at
     the view! What comfortable space for gathering!" And then the blessing
     began, *May this room bring people together, may it be a place of laughter and
     conversation, of quiet thoughts and sunlit reading.*
         We . . . *excuse me, pardon me, here we go* . . . moved to the bedroom
     and surrounded her bed. "For restful sleep!" one person said, as we all
     grunted and nodded and sighed our agreement. *For peace and comfort.
     For dreams, and memories, and waking refreshed to new days.*
         Then all eleven of us jammed ourselves into the otherwise spacious
     bathroom. After some giggling we settled in. We noted how bath-
     rooms see us as we really are, and how they are an intimate space
     where we are alone with our thoughts and we care for our bodies, a
     room of honesty and vulnerability. Then these ladies had practical
     blessings, such as a blessing for not slipping. We blessed the kitchen,
     for sharing food and welcoming guests, for nourishing our bodies and
     holding treasures passed down and gifts baked up. The women amped
     up as they went, thinking of more blessings, getting into it, and Marge
     in her blessed apartment beamed, and the moment itself felt so blessed.
     We ended in a circle in the living room once again, thanking God for
     our friend Marge, for her new home, and for the chapter closing and
     the chapter beginning, and for what God had in store for her in this
     new space. We gave her a plant as a tangible and visual blessing and
     reminder of her belovedness. And we all left feeling blessed.

Gather in the main room of the house.

Welcome those who gather and declare your intentions to bless this space.

Bless the room

Dipping a finger into the prepared oil, anoint the doorpost of the room, making the sign of the cross, say,
In the name of the Father, the Son, and the Holy Spirit.

Speak out intentions for this room.
What kind of life will happen in here?
Brainstorm together.
Bless the space by naming its purpose and what experiences and expressions of life this spaced will hold.

Prayer
When you are finished sharing, pray this prayer:
God, thank you for this room,
for all the life that has unfolded here before us,
and for all the life that is to come.
Fill this space with your light and your love.
Drive out all darkness and anything that
would hinder your love.

Bless those who come into this space.
And as we live in this room,
may our hearts be ever open to you.
Amen.

Move into the next room and repeat the process.

PART FOUR

Receiving What God Has Already Done

EIGHTEEN

Judgment: Letting Go of Condemnation

R ecently I said something thoughtless and careless in conversation that, if overheard, could have wounded someone deeply. Afterwards I was ashamed, flooded with guilt, horror, and regret. I also plunged into a good eight-hour session of relentless self-judgment and hearty self-condemnation. Even when I recognized I was caught in a loop, even when I tried to offer myself grace or remind myself of God's forgiveness, nothing I did or said to myself could break me free from my persistent self-denunciation. I was stuck in a cycle of judgment and condemnation, recognizing that what I did was wrong, and denouncing *myself* as wrong.

I wonder what Paul would think of our culture today. When he says, "There is therefore now no condemnation for those who are in Christ Jesus" (Rom 8:1), I think, *Sure, Paul, but have you seen us?* We are condemnation experts, condemnation ninjas—fast and skillful, stealthy and lethal with our condemnation talents. We're experienced professionals at denouncing one another and sheer geniuses at disowning ourselves. With swiftness and ease, we abolish people's belonging and eliminate their personhood. We dole out condemnation for what we do wrong, what we forget to do, and what we do right if we do it for the wrong reasons or use the wrong words. We can even time-travel our condemnation. We condemn people for things they said or did years ago, or for not coming clean in the present about things they said or did years ago. And we condemn ourselves for not knowing *then* what we know *now*, or even not knowing *yet* what we may know *eventually*.

We actually wake up and go into the world ready to condemn. From the mildly irritating in our own homes to the truly evil in our country, we find disagreeable people everywhere doing appalling things, and we are primed to notice and ready to condemn them. And we even help each other practice! The internet is filled with videos and descriptions of people behaving badly, dutifully recorded and shared online so the rest of us can condemn this person too.

We'd probably have to sit Paul down and explain to him, *Paul, dear, modern people believe it's our right, in fact, our duty, to "call out" others. And those who have done something especially offensive to us or awful to others should be rigorously condemned, which we today call "canceled."* Canceled *basically means life really would be better if this person didn't even exist.*

We see judgment and condemnation as the same thing. So here's where it gets tricky, because our culture says, "Don't judge." And we all live a bit terrified of being judged by others because we think that judgment has condemnation's power to erase, denounce, dehumanize, or damn us. *So,* we'd explain to Paul, *if you are going to live here with us, you will have to strive to be what we call "nonjudgmental" while also being quick to judge and roundly condemn those who judge others, all the while insisting you are* not *judgmental. The rules are a bit complicated, Paul, but you'll figure it out.*

But here's our problem: we are wired for judgment. We need judgment to make good decisions. We have to be able to size up situations and immediately assess our danger or safety, whether something is trustworthy or untrue, how best to respond to someone in need or react to someone's request. Good judgment is what keeps us from ingesting questionable things, driving reckless speeds, jumping from, balancing on, or plunging into deadly situations. Human beings need judgment. In fact, those with poor judgment or no judgment don't often live very long.

So we can't really escape judgment, nor, apparently, should we. But clearly, like smoke and fire, where there is judgment, there is condemnation. And here we are, participating in the whole vicious cycle. Just trying not to live in self-condemnation won't keep that from happening, and it's impossible to try not to judge each other. Especially when we're convinced that so many people around us are complete morons.

We are stuck. And as Paul himself says, there's nothing we can do to get ourselves unstuck (Rom 7:11–20). Just knowing what's right doesn't mean we'll do it, and besides, concentrating intensely on doing it right is another way of being stuck. And then Paul tells us, "There is therefore now no condemnation for those who are in Christ Jesus" (8:1). How can this be?

In Christ Jesus, God became a person, just like us, with us. God affirms personhood by taking on personhood and sharing our place as persons, with and for each other. In this way God makes personhood the place of holy encounter with the Divine. By coming as Christ incarnate to enter into our brokenness and division, *God* exercised the power to condemn. But what God condemns is *not* you or me, not vast groups of people, or people who do certain things or don't believe certain things. God does not condemn *people* at all; God affirms people. What God condemns— denounces, abolishes, banishes—is our division, our broken relationship with God and each other, anything we think has the power to harm and separate us. *God condemns the things that take away our personhood.*

By affirming persons and condemning what degrades our personhood, God does something remarkable. God separates condemnation from judgment. God redeems the purpose of judgment. Instead of making the law—an ethical framework for judging right and wrong—a means of condemnation, God makes it a means of grace. The judgment of God comes in grace. It comes to us as persons and calls us back to our personhood. God's judgment reveals the places of death in us or between us so that God's Spirit can make us alive. We can receive judgment instead of fearing it because judgment uncovers our jealousy, pride, or self-hatred. It reveals where we are dishonoring one another and causing harm.

We can even judge ourselves with God's judgment—without condemnation. God's judgment digs the person—whom God unequivocally upholds—out from under the dehumanizing and damaging behavior, words, attitudes and actions—which God staunchly condemns—setting the person free again. This judgment comes with grace that meets us in our stuckness with the possibility of healing and transformation, and both invites and empowers us to live differently.

And so, Paul—and we—can say with confidence that there is now, therefore, no condemnation for those who are in Christ Jesus. No condemnation. Not of myself, not of others. Dehumanizing others and dismissing them as worthless, overlooking those in need, calling out and labeling people (even ourselves) as monsters, idiots, or enemies—that will not stand. That has been put to death in Christ. That is sin, which God condemns. Labeling and dismissing people ignores their personhood, their humanity, when those very people belong to God and to all others. And that way of being doesn't control us anymore; we've been set free. When we are in Christ Jesus, Jesus's connection to God and all others is now ours. God makes it possible for us to live in our complete belonging to God and each other, which cannot be shaken.

So there is no condemnation for us, or in us, or through us, because condemnation of people has been condemned, and we have been made alive to belonging. Every time we condemn others or ourselves, we violate the fundamental belonging to God and each other that defines us as people. But we have been freed to honor and uphold all personhood. So you and I can walk into a situation and use judgment to see what is hurtful and what is good, what sows division and what affirms connection. We *must* judge so we can live in our true connection to God and each other, so we can see and value each other's personhood.

In Christ Jesus there is no condemnation, except the condemnation of our disconnection from God and one another. We human beings live free from condemnation and reserve condemnation for the things that strip people of their personhood. We are free to notice and judge when our own behavior is dehumanizing to others so we can change it. We are free not to participate in a tragic culture of constant condemnation. Instead of the Way of Fear, we live in the Way of God: we practice our belonging.

What an invitation, then! Whenever we feel the urge to condemn—whenever we feel tempted to see anyone as less than a beloved child of God, less than our sibling in this life—we can stop and take a beat, and remember that not only is condemnation not a right, but it's a violation of personhood, ours and theirs. We are in Christ Jesus, and there is no condemnation for those who are in Christ Jesus.

Instead, the Holy Spirit makes us able to look at each person with compassion and curiosity, to look again until we can see their personhood, to look until we can recognize our shared humanity and uphold them.[1] We look until we can say, *Here is a person who shares my humanity. Here is one of God's beloved with the same feelings and needs I have. Here is someone who gets lonely, sad, or desperate. Here is someone with loved ones and dreams and hopes. Here is someone who*

---

1   For victims of rape, incest, and abuse, this is a painfully difficult and slow process that should not be rushed or directed by others.

has suffered, perhaps someone whose behavior at the moment is what nonviolent communication might call "the tragic expression of unmet needs" or what makes Southerners say, "Bless their heart."

We are not permitted to dehumanize anyone, to dismiss or strip humanity away from anyone, not even ourselves. For us there is now therefore no condemnation. Instead, we receive the compassionate judgment of God, which releases us from condemnation, and we can opt out of the cultural condemnation game, that impossible dance happening all around us that operates as though condemnation and judgment were synonymous. God restores to us the use of sound judgment, calls us to uphold the personhood of all, and sets us free to live into our belonging to God in Christ and to all others.

When I realized I was stuck in a terrible cycle of condemnation, I could not free myself. I craved confession and absolution. Without knowing it at the time, what I was really wanting was judgment. I wanted to go find a Catholic church and put myself into a confessional booth and say what I'd done and hear through a small window words of grace spoken over me by a priest. Instead, I asked Andy to take a walk with me.

Because there was no way to confess my carelessness and harmful words to my friend without causing pain to them, I asked if I could confess to Andy. Believing in the priesthood of all believers means we can do this for one another, so I asked if he would be willing to hear me and offer me absolution. Then I told him what I had said. I let God's judgment rise up in me and name my words as wrong. I recognized my comments as a violation of my relationship with my friend and dehumanizing to myself. He listened. He agreed with me that what I said was wrong. We let the judgment stand. Together we condemned those words.

Then he gave me compassion and understanding. He saw my person underneath this act I regretted, and he upheld my personhood. He invited me into gentleness for myself. He pointed out the way my own recognition of my act was inviting me to talk and act in the future with more care and intention that reflected who I was and how I wanted to live. And then, as absurd as it sounds in today's modern world, he declared to me that I was forgiven. And I received this absolution. I let in his words. The condemnation slipped away, and I felt myself breathe again.

NINETEEN

Freedom: Letting Go of Ego

We're so far removed now from the intensity of the early days of the global Covid-19 pandemic, the weirdness of total lockdown, the constant unease and foreboding, and the excruciating unknown we endured every day as things gradually opened up, that we may barely remember what it was like, or how vigilantly we held to our positions even when we didn't really know what was going on. Six months into the pandemic, when some businesses and services were just reopening but many remained closed, I took my son to the barber. The sign on the door said masks were required. Inside with us were two barbers and one other client, all wearing masks. Then there was one barber without a client and without a mask. In this small space, he talked and talked and talked, loudly. We'd all just learned that the virus spread through aerosols, and I imagined his aerosols billowing through the air surrounding us all. I sat rigid, rage roiling inside me. How could he be breaking the rule posted on the door? Didn't he care about anyone else? What arrogance! What selfishness!

For a half hour, I wrestled with my anger and tried to get through my fierce judgment (condemnation!) to some empathy for myself and for him. I stoked my courage and practiced my words, and when Owen's haircut was finished, I told him to wait in the car. Heart pounding, I was about to say something to him when the man stood, put on a mask, and welcomed in his next masked client. I was shaking when I paid our barber, and I weakly told him I had been really uncomfortable that the other barber had not been wearing a mask.

This is just one of my many mighty mask moments. I almost never said something in real life to the actual person, but I spent more hours than I care to acknowledge having those conversations in my head—even going so far as to mentally design a card I might keep a stack of in my purse to somehow pass to the offending person informing them of the importance of mask-wearing while staying six feet away from them. I didn't have a lot of energy for much else in life right at the moment, but wow, could I find energy for this.

There are two ways to be free. Martin Luther and Dietrich Bonhoeffer distinguish between false freedom, which is *free from*, and true freedom, which is *free for*. We are free *for* each other, free *for* God, free *for* life. In Romans 6:15–23 Paul says, essentially, *You can live in your freedom, not bound by anything or anyone. You can act as though you are a sovereign entity, free from others. But all that gets you is more isolation and deadness. To pretend we are not connected violates our very being and dehumanizes others.*

To be free, then, as Paul describes it, means our lives are ruled not by our own self-determination but by being children of God who belong to each other. By that token, in the midst of a deadly pandemic, wearing a mask is a simple way to live in real freedom. We don't wear it for ourselves; we wear it to protect each other. We wear it to contribute to well-being for one another, for all.

Except here's the thing. In the moment when I was dutifully wearing my mask and someone near me was not, I did not feel free. I felt trapped in anger and despair. And I didn't even want to be *for* them! I wanted to be free *from* them! Free from their selfishness, from the risk they were creating, free from the consequences of their actions in our society—the extension of this pandemic. In fact, I wanted so badly to be free from the pandemic itself that anyone I saw as working against that goal felt like an enemy.

And besides, if I wore a mask, I got to show that I was on the right side of things. I got to show that I cared about others, whereas, clearly, they did not.

And suddenly this action that should be about belonging to each other becomes about condemnation and self-justification, and it contributes to greater division and contempt. And now Paul would lump me right into his definition of sin that violates my own humanity and denies others, and say I am living under the law and not under grace.

So what does real freedom look like?

In the first century something happened to the Christian church that exploded its numbers and transformed the community from a small, obscure sect to a movement big enough to eventually be noticed by Constantine and ultimately made into the official religion of the Roman Empire. That something was an epidemic.

When a plague came to Rome, everyone with any means—even the doctors—left the city and went to the Italian countryside to protect themselves. They exercised their personal freedom from constraints and got themselves out of harm's way.

Except the poor and the sick could not leave; they were forced to stay. So the Christians stayed too, and cared for them. Christian women, in particular, nursed the sick. Two things resulted. The first is that compassion was revealed as central to the message of this new religion. Compassion became a calling, nursing the sick a mark of the Christian church—which, in part, is why Christianity is responsible for the creation of more hospitals than any other institution or group.

But second, mysteriously, many of these Christians didn't die. It seemed to the rest of the society that they were inexplicably and supernaturally protected from death. That may be. It's also likely they developed immunity that allowed them to keep nursing the weak. And these women could trust that if they were to fall ill, they too would be nursed.

They did not stay behind to care for the vulnerable because they thought the plague was fake, or that God would protect them and not others, or because they wanted to prove they were better than other people. They put themselves at risk to care for the vulnerable because they believed the only way we are truly alive, truly free, is to live free *for* our neighbor, free *for* the most vulnerable and weakest among us. Plague or no plague, we belong to God and each other.

This is the deepest mark of the Christian. These Christians were so intriguing to the greater populace because they seemed to be without fear—even fear of dying. According to Paul, we have already died with Christ and been raised to new life. In life and in death we belong to God (Rom 14:8, and *A Brief Statement of Faith*, PC[USA]). No matter what, our true life is found in connection to God and each other.

True freedom extends deep and wide. Whatever the behavior of others or the circumstances around us, we can still be free. We are free to love and serve and care for each other. We are free to honor our limitations as human beings, free to rest when we are tired, free to say we need help, free to receive support from others, and free to give support to others. We are free to receive criticism from others without dread that it will destroy us. We are free to speak out when we see harm being done to another person, and free to repent, confess, and ask forgiveness when our words or actions harm another person. We are free to face our complicity in racism and look at our history with unflinching gaze and grief that could open us up to a new way. We are free to have our prejudices dismantled and to be surprised by one another's humanity. We are free to reestablish broken relationships and revisit regrets for doorways to new life. There are no sides in the kingdom of God. There is just broken and beloved humanity, all of us, belonging always to a steadfast and faithful God.

When we try to live free *from* God and others, we are instead ruled by our egos, by the need to earn or prove something. Or we are bound to act out of obligation and duty, or dominated by anger or contempt. But when we surrender to our weakness and stuckness, what we thought was freedom is exposed as chains, and we find our true freedom not in what we do for ourselves, or in what others do or don't do, but in what Christ has done for us all. We die to sin and are made alive to our true humanity in Christ. We are set free to live toward each other and toward God. In Christ, God reconciled the world to Godself and entrusted us with the message of reconciliation (2 Cor 5:19). We are free to live into and out of this belonging to God and each other.

A half hour after leaving the barber shop, I got a text from an unknown number. "Hi, is this Kara? This is Chris, the owner of the barber shop. I want to apologize for not wearing my mask today when you were in the shop. I completely understand and sincerely apologize. I had gotten into the habit of pulling my mask down between appointments and feel awful if I made you uncomfortable while you were in today. I hope you can accept my apology and know that I do sincerely apologize."

I was surprised and flooded with gratitude. I could have been *free from* him. I was "free" to leave the shop and never go back. Good riddance! I had struggled so hard to find my humanity and his in the midst of that, to stay in (at least the concept of) our belonging to each other, which demands we see and hear the other, and saying something to our barber about my experience was the closest I could get. I mostly still felt trapped in anger, stuck in condemnation and anxiety.

Barbershop Chris had his freedom too. He could have been *free from* me. He could have written me off and never given me a second thought. But instead he was free *for* me. He acted from our mutual belonging and reached out. And when he was free for me, he helped me be free too. We were both reconciled to the freedom of our true humanity.

I texted back my gratitude, and we wished one another well. And I took a deep breath and thanked God for the way Christ had met me in Chris.

Life is messy, and being human is hard. May we be ruled by freedom to be with and for each other. May we be freed from ego and returned to our true belonging.

TWENTY

Forgiveness: Letting Go

When I was a kid, I was happy to be dragged around the country to different camps and church events where my dad would speak to the grown-ups and my mom would lead "creative dramatics" with the kids. Essentially, this meant acting out Bible stories from a set of rhyming storybooks she brought along. The parable we call "The Unforgiving Servant" (Matt 18:21–35) is one that I acted out so many times as a kid, with so many groups of strangers, that I can still remember the exact lines that once got me kicked out of the room.

In this parable Jesus tells the story of a king who forgives a servant's debt, the equivalent of 200,000 days' work. The king forgives it all. And then the delighted servant leaves, a free man, and immediately bumps into someone who owes him a small amount of money (half of 1 percent of what the servant owed the king). The servant seizes him by the throat and demands payment, and when the debtor cannot pay, he throws his fellow servant into jail. The king catches wind of the man's actions and orders he be tortured until his original, impossible debt is paid.

My mom was reading the story, doing the voices of the characters, and fifty children were sitting cross-legged and rapt. We were getting to my favorite part. I had surreptitiously positioned my seven-year-old self right next to her, almost facing the rest of the kids. My heart was pounding wildly as I worked up my courage for a surprise assist. The moment came, and she read, "'How much does he owe?' The king asked the treasurer, standing below."

And I roared out the answer at the top of my lungs, *"TEN THOUSAND!"*

My mom was supposed to continue, "The treasurer's answer was loud! 'Ten thousand!?' exclaimed everyone in the crowd." But instead the air in the room turned electric at my outburst, and all eyes swiveled to me, wide and worried. My mother, misreading my helpful contribution as impertinent disrespect, aimed a stiff and shaking arm at the door, finger pointed like a sharp arrow, and said in a voice quivering with fury, "OUT!"

Horrified, I stood and slunk out to the hallway, where I wept bitterly.

We like to turn parables into morality tales with which to either smack ourselves or pat our own backs. Hearing this story maybe one hundred times in my childhood gave me plenty of chances to feel either mildly convicted that I wasn't more forgiving to my sisters or classmates, or smug that I wasn't like this total fool of a servant who couldn't appreciate the great good fortune he'd been given. But Jesus doesn't tell parables to slightly alter our behavior or congratulate us. He tells parables with absurd extremes to reveal how we're living trapped in the Way of Fear instead of free in the Way of God. And forgiveness is not something to measure ourselves by; rather, it's a way of receiving and sharing in the life we've been given.

But forgiveness is not easy. The parable is told in response to a very valid question Peter asks. He has been listening to all Jesus's teaching about conflict and forgiveness and thinks to himself, *Over and over and over again I go through the work of forgiving someone who hurts me. So when is enough? When can I stop? How much am I expected to put up with?* Then, maybe stretching to the outer limits of his capacity, he suggests an answer—a good, large, and even holy-sounding number: *How about seven times? Surely that is a beyond-generous amount. Right, Jesus?*

And Jesus tells him, *Try seventy times that.* In other words—infinity times, Peter. Just keep on going till you lose track. There is no end to forgiveness. No point at which you've reached the limit. No strikes or chances, no lifetime maximum out-of-pocket amount. Then, to drive the point home, he tells the parable of the unforgiving servant.

The Greek word we translate as "forgiveness" means simply "to let go." But that's not so simple. Sometimes we see this letting go as letting someone get away with something or acting like what happened wasn't significant. We feel loyal to our pain. We stroke it and stoke it, longing for our injury to be recognized as unjust and wrong, and act as though to forgive someone else is to somehow betray ourselves.

Our culture at the moment is particularly unforgiving. Instead of showing mercy, which is defined as "compassion or forgiveness . . . toward someone whom it is within one's power to punish or harm,"[1] we seem to want to *punish* all those within our power to punish. We're much more the servant than the king (at least in the first part of the story). Generally speaking, we are all for forgiveness, most of the time. Only, some people, we like to tell ourselves, don't *deserve* forgiveness.

But *forgiveness* isn't in the same zip code as *deserve.* They are completely different languages, contradictory accounting systems. *Forgive* and *deserve* are more like opposites, since forgiveness frees us from a system of gauging and measuring and puts us instead into the realm of boundless and unlimited love.

Forgiving sweeps the built-up resentment out of our souls and announces to all who will listen that past suffering, pain, betrayal, or burdens won't entrap us or shape

1   *Oxford English Dictionary,* s.v. "mercy."

our future. Those who have injured us can't redefine us by their actions. Forgiveness declares that the future will not be determined by the past. Biblical scholar Craig Koester says, "Forgiveness opens up a future that the past has closed off."[2] Forgiveness means our identity is shaped by our belovedness instead of our woundedness. Forgiveness is letting go.

But how in the world do we forgive?

Several years ago, I heard a talk by Dr. Fred Luskin, a world expert on forgiveness and director of the Stanford Forgiveness Project.[3] He shared that his work began out of frustration that most faith traditions speak extensively about the need to forgive and how good it is to do, but they don't tell us *how* to forgive. They don't often help us forgive; they just tell us it is important. And people get so stuck in unforgiveness. So very stuck. So, he began to study it. And by the time I heard him speak, he had dedicated twenty-five years of research and work to teaching people how to forgive and to measuring scientifically the effect it has on people's bodies and minds and relationships. And do you know what his team has discovered is at the very root of all forgiveness?

Abiding in God's love.

Of course, they wouldn't say it that way in the laboratory. Instead, they would talk about finding that place of peace within, about living from that place. But the way you get there? Love. He walked us through an example. "Think of someone you adore," he said. "Get a good picture of them in your head. Remember what it feels like to be so

---

2   Craig Koester, "NL Podcast 353: Forgiveness," March 2, 2019, in *Narrative Lectionary*, https://tinyurl.com/ysdmdtsz.

3   Fred Luskin, "The Power of Forgiveness," Westminster Town Hall Forum, May 5, 2011, https://tinyurl.com/yc6pnpje.

loved by them, so known and valued.[4] How they delight in you!

"Breathe deeply. Let your heart even get warm right now as you think of this person. Hold that feeling within you.

"Now open your eyes," he said. "Five minutes of this every day is more effective than psychotherapy in helping people to forgive."

Love unclenches our heart. Love drives out fear and frees us—ever so much more—to forgive and to live even more out of the love that holds us, because all forgiveness, all love and mercy and with-each-other-ness, come from God's own love, God's own being.

When the dead and risen Jesus comes to the scared and confused disciples, he says, "Peace be with you" (John 20:21–23). Then he says, "Receive the Holy Spirit," and like shivers down the spine, the Breath of Life breathes life on them. *Take in the life of the Giver of Life. Let it stir you alive as it did the creature,* Adam, *from the earth,* adamah, *as it hovered over the waters when there was nothing but emptiness, moving the nascent world into vibrant, joyful being.*

And then he speaks these words to them: "If you forgive the sins of any, they are forgiven them; if you retain the sins of any, they are retained." *You are now in this peace with me—this abiding in love and inviting others to abide there too, this trusting-God-for-life kind of living. You are drawn into the very relationship of God—the force that binds God and Jesus through the Holy Spirit, the inner substance of the Holy. And in this love you have power. If you want to hang onto the things that divide and destroy, hold them, and they will be held. But if you let them go, if you release them, they are gone. This is your calling in the world, to live from this love; to be grudge-releasers and mercy-sharers and trusters*

---

4   Thank you to Pastor Antoinette Moss, who points out this practice is reminiscent of Phil 4:8–9.

of love and dwellers in peace and spreaders of forgiveness and hope; to live inside my connection to God and all others. To let God's life flow through you. Love each other.

As those defined by and following the Way of God, we've chosen a way of life that begins in abundance and sharing instead of earning and proving. A way of life expressed in generosity and care for one another instead of self-preservation and isolation. A life in which we see each other as beloved companions instead of calloused competition. This living begins in the very being of the One who embraces us and claims us, whose nature is love spilled out on us and lived out through us in the world.

As we abide in this way of life, forgiveness is the currency. Forgiveness is God's own lifeblood, poured out for us. It's how we remain free, how we receive the grace we're given, and how we go deeper toward the hope to which we are called in God. Forgiveness doesn't make us right or settle a score. It's not something people can deserve, earn, or lose. Our own forgivenness by God is how we experience our true humanity and how we live into it as children of this God whose being is love. We let go and we are held. Receiving our own forgivenness empowers our forgiveness.

The servant in the parable was forgiven more than he could repay in fifteen lifetimes and then immediately and violently demanded someone repay a debt to him. This is like celebrating sobriety with a drinking binge, like running back into the burning building you were just rescued from, like scrapping the Ten Commandments for the golden calf and pining for the enslavement of Egypt. He sticks with his old identity instead of the new one offered him by the king. He says, "Thanks, but no thanks" to a life of freedom and generosity, and chooses instead the way of debt and indebtedness, where people keep track and there is no forgetting, no forgiving, no freedom, no letting go.

Choose, then, with which currency you wish to live. Which way will define you and shape your life? If you choose a world without forgiveness, you choose to be chained to the suffering of the past. You choose to repeat old hurts and live them currently, to nurture and tend your pain, with no chance of release. Hanging onto wounds, insults, and offenses, practicing and spreading this pattern of deprivation and resentment, traps you ever more tightly in a misery of your own making.

So I can't help thinking Jesus told his parable to Peter with a twinkle in his eye, his words like a shove on Peter's shoulder, to highlight to him the absurdity of Peter's question:

> *How much forgiveness is enough, Jesus, before I can stop and be done with it already? How much freedom from injury do I have to endure before I get to be imprisoned in bitterness? At what point am I allowed to quit living in a future defined by love? Is seven times a sacrificial and generous amount of letting go before it's appropriate to throw in the towel and go back to hanging onto betrayal and stoking anger?*

Peter doesn't know what's coming—that Jesus will die and take into himself all suffering and betrayal, all pain and injustice; that none of it, ever, goes unseen, untended, unmet. God incarnate will bear it all, all that has been and all that will be. And as the last breath leaves his human body, Jesus will look out at his murderers and whisper, "Father, forgive them. They don't know what they're doing" (Luke 23:34, my paraphrase). And they will cease being those who are killing God and instead become those on whom God has poured unending love.

Jesus will die in freedom and release his killers—and all of us as well, taking into the heart of God all the terrible things we think and say and do to one another, everything, every one of us. Setting aside deserve and debt, punishment and payback, Jesus will open to us mercy, grace, forgiveness, and freedom. All that is dead—between us, within us, around us—is swallowed up by resurrection. Our brokenness is now the ground from which new life is born, green, beautiful, and eternal.

We get to put down our burdens. Let them go. Christ has taken them up. In exchange for our woundedness, he hands us belovedness. This is what defines us now; this is our identity. Forgivenness is an invitation to let go of hanging on, and share in the being of God, and so to be truly alive.

TWENTY-ONE

Prayers for Receiving What God Has Already Done

PRAYER FOR JUDGMENT
WITHOUT CONDEMNATION

Lord, I am bound in condemnation.
I can feel it bubbling up, churning around,
    longing to spew.
I can condemn myself. I can condemn others.
With a flick of my mind,
I can condemn the world and everyone in it.
I'm that good at it.
Your word says there is no condemnation for those
    who are in Christ Jesus.
That's what I want. I want to be free.
Set me free.

Make me free for my neighbor,
free for connection,
free for clarity and purpose and love,
free for joy.
I want to be free to tell the truth,
free to speak out,
free to stay silent,
free to receive judgment that could set me free.

Make me free to forgive
And free to be forgiven and feel it.
Free me from condemnation, Lord.

This, I pray.
Then I remember:
I am already free.
There is no condemnation for those who are in
    Christ Jesus.

So help me live my freedom.
Redeem my judgment.

Give me wisdom and discernment.
Give me insight and understanding.

And if not those things,
then give me Pause,
So I may listen instead of speaking,
observe instead of assuming,
be present instead of dismissing,
and learn to live,
one thought at a time,
into freedom.
Amen.

NIGHT PRAYER FOR RELEASE FROM FALSE FREEDOM

O Lord, release me from false freedom this night,
and bring me to wholeness and life in the new day.

Release me from judgment and fear,
make me free for curiosity and compassion.

Release me from anger and despair,
make me free for mourning and trust.

Release me from comparison and striving,
make me free for generosity and ease.

Release me from isolation and self-preservation,
make me free for connection and belonging.

May I seek your face in the faces of others.
May I find my place here among all others.

Lead me through death to new life again, O God.
Rest me in you this night.

Awaken me in you in the new day.
Amen.

A PRAYER FOR THE ANXIOUS

God, fear is peddled in the streets,
    on our screens, over our airwaves.
It's the poison in the air that is making us sick.

The infection distorts our view—
making neighbor seem like enemy,
fellow human being like a threat.

The illness warps our thinking—
making us desperate for safety,
and willing to sacrifice love, joy, peace, patience,
    kindness, generosity, and self-control
in order to get it.

The disease dulls our senses—
to the beauty, the interconnectedness,
    the hope, the promise
always lurking
in every interaction, every silence,
the laughter and tears, the hugs and hands touching.

There it is: the truth,
    plugging along its steady course,
life, persistent
in brilliant tree and scurrying squirrel,
in squealing baby and sleeping dog,
all of whom are unaffected completely
by politics, prognostication, and posturing,
all of whom remember who they are
and whose they are.

You are God.
Here yesterday, here today, and here tomorrow.
You are the source of all things,
the creator of love, the bringer of peace,
    the giver of patience,
met in each kindness, and celebrated in each
    generosity.

"You are gifts to each other," you say to us.
"This life is a gift."

Heal us from this malady.
Cleanse us
and restore our souls to health.

Rest us
so we can awaken into
truth, and there abide—
truth that "this too shall pass,"
but also truth that this will remain:
We all belong to you. We all belong to each other.
Amen.

EXPECTING EPIPHANY—A PRAYER FOR OPENNESS

*May be used in worship on/during Epiphany. Pronouns may
be made plural for group prayer.*

God, open me to the mystery of your presence
    in my life.
Open me to your light in the world.
Move me beyond the religious definitions,
    boundaries, and explanations

---

that are holding me back from your broader love,
your brighter light, your deeper purpose,
and your insistence on involving me
in a tale I can't imagine,
a wonder that wants to dislodge me from my tedium
and thrust me into anticipation.

Show me how I am connected
to you
to others
to a calling beyond myself.
Teach me to expect epiphany.
Amen.

YOUR LAW IN MY HEART—A PRAYER OF GRATITUDE

"I delight to do your will, O my God;
　　your law is within my heart." (Ps 40:8)

I love to do your will, O God.
I love to feel myself part of the fabric of life.
I love sensing my connection to other people.
I love being awake
to life, to gratitude, to joy,
to being rolled by laughter,
washed by tears,
summoned by a sunset,
moved by a mountain,
and stirred by a song.
Your way is inside me, God.
It's part of me,
leading me,
and leading me back when I lose my way,

leading me home again.
Amen.

LORD, I AM WEAK—A PRAYER OF CONFESSION

Lord, I am weak.
I am incapable of trusting, unable to live in freedom,
and I keep on choosing bondage instead of life.

But I see the power of your love.
I see what forgiveness releases and what hope ignites.
I have experienced your grace
and I want to be part of it with my whole being.

Instead of fear, I want faith to tell me what is real.
I want my life to participate—
to grieve and forgive
and set free and heal
and welcome and repent
and witness your redemption every single day.
Lord, use me.

Help me to trust in your faithfulness.
Help me to believe
that you always bring life out of death,
and to trust
that you will bring life from the death
within and around me
right now.

Connect again my being to your own,
that I may know you love me
and that my life may flow from that truth.
Amen.

A PRAYER FOR A DIFFICULT PERSON

(Pronouns can be made plural; maybe you need this prayer for a whole group of people.)

God, this person is driving me nuts.
I don't understand them.
I don't want to understand them.
They're wrong, and that's the end of it.

God, this person is your beloved child.
You claim them as your own.
You gave me to them
and them to me
in this human family.
I do not get to dismiss them
or be free of them.

I lift to you, Lord,
my unmet need for shared reality.
Oh, that we could see the world the same way!
Oh, that there could be
ease and unity,
trust and mutuality!

I grieve, God, that this does not seem possible.
Help me to grieve.
Take my anger, Lord.
Replace my frustration with compassion.

Beyond this disagreement,
show me how
their longing to be seen and known is just like mine,
their wanting to live a good life is just like mine,

their childhood hurt, and teenage mistakes,
    and adult heartbreak
are just like mine.
Remind me that
the circumstances they have experienced,
suffering they have endured,
events that have shaped them,
I can know nothing about.

They are mystery to me,
as I am mystery to them,
and you are mystery to us both.
Help me to honor the shared humanity
and the sacred mystery of this person
I am struggling to understand.

Help me let go of my need for them to change
and learn to accept them as they are.
Teach me to honor the mix
    of disappointment and longing
that rises up in me when I see them,
without trying to escape my discomfort.
And then, help me to love them
without strings or conditions.

And if I am wrong, show me my wrong.
And if I am right, help me to rest in you anyway,
and not in my own rightness.
Because next time, I may very well be wrong,
and right now,
someone may be praying this prayer
about me.
Amen.

A PRAYER FOR FORGIVENESS BEFORE SLEEPING

God, I pause at the end of this day
to let my awareness catch up with me.
I can see the sin and brokenness within me.
I don't turn away but welcome that awareness now,
and name now those places in me where I long for
    your healing and wholeness. . . .
(needs within are lifted up)
Lord, have mercy.
Christ, have mercy.

God, I welcome awareness of the sin and brokenness
in my relationships with those close to me
and those I don't know so well.
Into all the ways I act as though
    we do not belong to each other,
bring your healing and wholeness, especially . . .
(needs between are lifted up)
Lord, have mercy.
Christ, have mercy.

God, I welcome awareness of the sin and brokenness
    around me.
I lift up those places in my community,
my country,
and your world,
where I long for your healing and wholeness,
    especially . . .
(wider needs are lifted up)
Lord, have mercy.
Christ, have mercy.

Hold me in your forgiveness.
Speak to me your peace.

Rest me in your grace.
Amen.

GOD IS OUR KEEPER—A PRAYER

A prayer with optional sung response, such as Be Still and Know That I Am God *or another Taizé song. (words of the people in bold)*

God, you are our keeper. With you, nothing is lost.
We pray for lost things—
lost dreams, lost loved ones,
lost understandings of ourselves.
We pray for those we know who are lost
and for all those who've lost home and safety.
To you, O Lord, we lift our hearts.
Sung response

God, you are our keeper. You tend us.
Clean out the parts of us that need cleansing.
Pull the weeds and turn the soil of our souls.
Mend our broken hearts and places of wounding.
Heal our relationships and division.
To you, O Lord, we lift our hearts.
Sung response

God, you are our keeper. You sustain us and maintain us on our way.
Keep our hearts in your love and safety.
Keep our minds in the truth.
Keep our hands in your work.
Keep our feet on your path.
Keep our souls in your joy.
Keep us in your care.

To you, O Lord, we lift our hearts.
Sung response
Amen.

A PRAYER FOR ELECTION DAY—A LITANY FOR THE FOURTH OF JULY

To use this prayer for the Fourth of July, delete the words in italics and replace with the words in [brackets].

We belong
first and foremost
to you, Lord.
God of heaven and earth,
eternity and the moment,
ever and always.

Then we belong to the whole of creation.
the living, the dead,
the yet-to-become and the reborn,
the whole ongoing cycle of earth and life
with all its glorious array of ever-expanding participants:
mountains and trees and oceans and valleys,
gazelles and robins and rivers and earthworms,
all.

Next we belong to the human family,
all humanity in every corner of the vast globe
all languages, creeds, cultures, skin tones, religions,
        beliefs, experiences, hopes, celebrations,
        losses, goals, vocations, technologies, and
        connections,
in grief and wonder and anger and happiness and
        confusion and sadness and joy,
whatever happens and no matter what

—we belong to them all, all, all.
And they all
belong to us.

After this, we are grouped—
some arbitrarily and some by choice—
into land masses and geographic regions.
We develop identifying accents, clothing preferences,
    and regional tastebuds,
which is to say we gather our experiences into
    ourselves
alongside others
who are gathering into themselves experiences
alongside us.

We call our places of belonging towns, counties,
    villages, and cities,
tribes, nations, countries, continents, and
    coalitions.
These countless designations simply mean that
we live nearby and agree to certain codes of living
    with one another
that in one way or another uphold our greater
    belonging—
to the whole human family, the living and the dead
    of all creation,
and the Lord of all.

Next are the smaller groups in which we learn
and the people there who teach us,
the neighbors, musicians, coaches, and collaborators,
the members of our faith, our teams, our clans.
We have hobbies we cultivate with the people who
    practice them alongside us,
passions we pursue and those whom they impact,

jobs we end up in with those who end up there too,
whose lives intertwine with our own.

And then there are those specific people from whom
        we come,
the ones whose being and belonging
shape our own being and belonging most directly.
I mean, of course,
our ancestors and grandparents,
aunts and uncles, cousins and kin,
parents and siblings.

We may have the partner with whom we share our life,
and the children whom we shape and watch become,
and the pets we collect into our homes,
and the gardens we tend,
and the friendships we cultivate,
and the places we grow our roots,
deep, strong, and sure,
with and for those to whom we give our hearts,
who will one day be buried in the ground alongside
        everyone and everything else
to which we already and always belong.

So, on this day, *when our democracy is verbed*
And we exercise our right and responsibility to
        participate together
In shaping the future of our shared home [that cele-
        brates our nation],
we give thanks for all the belongings that hold and
        shape us,
both created and innate.

We give thanks for the communities into which we
        pour our lives
and for all those in our communities who pour their
        lives into us.

We give thanks for the earth that nurtures all life
and for all those who nurture the earth.

On this day that *shapes* [celebrates] our nation,
in our collective belonging called the United States
    of America
we give thanks for all that is good and wise and
    kind,
all that upholds our humanity,
both individual and shared.
Thank you, God.

And in our collective belonging called the United
    States of America
we confess all that is evil, foolish, and divisive,
all that damages our soul,
both individual and shared.
Forgive us, Lord.

And when this day *of national weighing-in*
    [that celebrates our nation]
has come to an end,
and whatever comes next begins
    [in fireworks and fanfare],
it remains
that beyond country, beyond kin,
beyond borders and beliefs,
beyond any and all boundaries,
whether natural or unnatural,
is the Great Belonging,
that is,
to each other, all,
and to you, Lord of all.

For this, today,
we give thanks.
Amen.

HALLELUJAH FOR EASTER

Written to be sung to the tune of "Hallelujah" by Leonard Cohen.[1]

There is a story, and it's true,
of love that came for me and you,
And I am going to sing this story to ya
This story is for every heart,
And every person has a part,
So listen as I sing this Hallelujah

Hallelujah, hallelujah, hallelujah, hallelujah

From nothing all things came to be,
All color, light and harmony,
God exhaled beauty, joy and life right through ya
All things belonged, and all were one,
Till fear crept in to steal the throne,
And turned our hearts away from Hallelujah

Hallelujah, hallelujah, hallelujah, hallelujah

A baby born and laid in hay,
The one who made the night and day
You came to earth and let life happen to ya
With truth and hope in every call,
you loved and healed and welcomed all,
And every breath you drew was "Hallelujah"

Hallelujah, hallelujah, hallelujah, hallelujah

In fear they put you on the cross

---

1   An Easter morning staple for our congregation, sung for years by my
daughter, Maisy. Now sung by the whole congregation.

Our hope was gone, and all was lost
When death reached out and pulled the breath right
    from ya
The earth it shook, the sky turned dark,
Our brokenness pierced God's own heart,
The world was void of every hallelujah

Hallelujah, hallelujah, hallelujah, hallelujah

But at the end, it all begins,
Cause hope and love will always win,
And fear's no match for God's great claim upon ya
He rose from death to reign on high,
and raises us to love and life,
To lift our voices singing Hallelujah!

Hallelujah, hallelujah, hallelujah, hallelu . . .
Hallelujah, hallelujah, hallelujah, hallelujah.

TWENTY-TWO

Practices for Receiving What God Has Already Done

FREEDOM—A WALKING PRAYER

God is always beckoning us toward freedom. Sometimes we tell ourselves things are freedom that are not.

Walking In

As you walk, invite the Holy Spirit to show you what you could let go of to move to deeper freedom.

Don't stretch your brain to try to think of things. This is not a head exercise; it's a body and heart prayer. Simply seek to be open and receptive.

The Center

Pause. In the true center of your true self, you are already free.

That is, you are completely loved by and connected to God. This cannot be taken away and cannot be earned. It simply is. In the very end, this is what you will know forever and live in without hesitation.

Walking Out

Imagine yourself carrying that freedom within you into the world, wherever you go and whatever you do.

Again, don't strain your head. Simply seek to be open and receptive.

GOD KNOWS IT ALL, JESUS IS HERE—A PRAYER FOR OTHERS

God loves those you love and cares about those you are worried for. There is nothing they are going through that God does not see and know. If this prayer is for someone with whom you are angry, disappointed, or hurt, remember that there is nothing God does not see and know. Whoever they are and whatever the situation, Jesus is with them—whether they know it or not. God's mercy and grace is available to them and to you.

Light a candle to pray for someone.

Imagine God's reality—truthful, honest, seeing and knowing all, tender and full of mercy—is surrounding and holding them.

Imagine God's mercy and grace surrounding and filling you.

GOD KNOWS IT ALL, JESUS IS HERE—A PRAYER FOR THE WORLD

Praying for the world can be enriched and focused by viewing an image of the globe or a map.

Consider all the places and situations that we are bombarded with in the news or that weigh heavy on our hearts, all the suffering in the world, the dysfunction and systemic abuse, racism and corruption, those who've lost loved ones to sickness or fire or famine or flood, species dying out and the earth gasping for health. Do we sometimes feel like it's ours to carry or fix? Do we believe if we turn our eyes or thoughts away, we are abandoning our human siblings or our post as stewards of the earth?

Write on a sticky note, index cards, or slip of paper "GOD KNOWS IT ALL."

On a second, write "JESUS IS HERE."

Pick a place for which to pray. Hold one note in each hand.

Say, "God knows all that is happening here" and "Jesus is with these people right now." As you consider that place, read each message aloud to yourself: *God knows it all*, and *Jesus is here*.

Release the people, place, and situation to God.

Pick another place. Repeat until you feel complete.

Sit quietly in God's presence, meditating on the world. Imagine this world held in God's unending love. Imagine God's mercy and grace flowing to where it is needed.

OPEN TO FORGIVING—A PRAYER EXERCISE

Sit in a chair with an empty chair across from you. Imagine that sitting in that empty chair is someone you long to forgive. (This someone might be yourself.)

In your mind, describe the hurt.

What happened? Describe it simply and directly, without judgment or analysis. Get down to the bare facts, as best you can. If it helps, write down what occurred.

Now, take some time to rest in God's healing grace. Imagine how it will feel to have this burden lifted. Imagine the extra room in your heart. Imagine the lightness and ease in your body. Imagine your spirit set free. Imagine looking at the person in the chair across from you and seeing them in the light of compassion, grace, and freedom.

When you are ready, in the quiet of your heart, tell God that you are willing and ready to forgive.

You might want to do this with a simple breath prayer. Breathing in, in your mind say, "I am willing." Breathing out, say, "I am free." Or if you don't feel ready to forgive, breathe in: "I want to forgive." Breathe out: "Help me to want to forgive."

Before you go, if you are ready, say to the person in that chair across from you that the work of forgiveness has begun in you.
If you can, offer them peace.

ADMITTING WEAKNESS, RECEIVING GRACE—A WALKING PRAYER

You will need a heavy coat and a light, beautiful scarf or cloth.

Before God no creature is hidden; we all are our most naked selves, vulnerable and exposed, no pretending, no pretense, no armor. At the same time, in Christ God shares completely what it is to be human in every way, every challenge and struggle we face, yet without the barrier (i.e., sin) between God and us, or us and each other. So we can come to God with boldness. We will receive mercy, and we will find help in our need.

Walking In
Put on the heavy coat. (Keep the scarf in a pocket or carry it). Wear the coat as you walk.
What does it represent for you? What do you imagine keeps you from fully receiving God's love? What protection or armor do you put on to guard your vulnerable self? It may be stories

you tell yourself about your own worth; it may be comparisons to others

or to some standard out there. It may be things you think you are performing for God or for others.

Name those things to God as you walk.

The Center

Imagine arriving in God's presence, in the presence of complete love and acceptance—God who knows you fully and utterly.

Remove the heavy coat and all that it symbolizes to you. How does it feel to take it off? (Drop it in the center. If you are walking outdoors, you probably can't just leave it here, but see it as completely off of you, other than you.)

Receive the scarf or cloth and lay it on your shoulders. Imagine it as God's claim on you—God's mercy and grace surrounding you, gently resting on you as you walk back.

Walking Out

When you're ready, walk back out.

Imagine God's love and acceptance resting on you, filling you up, moving you back into your life without fear or judgment.

SUBMIT, RESIST, DRAW NEAR—A WALKING PRAYER

"Submit yourselves therefore to God. Resist the devil, and he will flee from you. Draw near to God, and he will draw near to you." (James 4:7–8)

Walking In: Submit to God

As you walk, imagine "submit yourself" as a gentle and loving invitation from God.

> What can you submit? Confess, lay down, surrender? Terrors? Worries? Exhaustion? Anger? The stories you are telling yourself about life or the future or your family? What if you opened up right now and just dumped all of it before God?

The Center: Resist the Accuser

When you arrive at the halfway (five-minute) point, imagine arriving in God's presence, in the presence of complete love and acceptance.

Breathe in the love of God.

> Imagine the love of God is pouring into your body and filling every part of you, from your toes to the top of your head.

Breathe out the love of God that has just filled you.

> Imagine it as a love force field, blocking the voice of accusation, condemnation, and blame coming at you or others. As you exhale the love of God that has filled you, imagine that love force field resisting the accuser, and the accusations crashing against it and dissipating into the air, dissolving into nothing.

Stand here for a couple minutes.

> Breathe in complete love and acceptance. Breathe out complete love and acceptance.

Walking Out: Draw Near to God

When you're ready, walk back held in God's love.

> Imagine God's love and acceptance as a bubble of light surrounding you, within you, radiating from you. Imagine you are actually held within the love of God. Your feet don't even touch the ground; the bubble of love holds you above, beneath, behind, and in front; inside and outside, God is carrying you.

SUBMIT, RESIST, DRAW NEAR— PRAYING FOR OTHERS

"Submit yourselves therefore to God. Resist the devil, and he will flee from you. Draw near to God, and he will draw near to you." (James 4:7–8)

Submit

Write down the name of someone you'd like to pray for, or speak it aloud to God and submit them to God.

Imagine God's reality—gentle, peaceable, full of mercy—is surrounding and filling them. Draw a heart around their name. Maybe even doodle "blessings" around their name.

Resist

If there are lies that you know they are telling themselves or absorbing (e.g., *I am trapped, I am not worthy of love, nobody cares,* and the like), acknowledge them to God.

If there are lies you are hearing about them, (e.g., *it's hopeless, God doesn't care,* and so forth), acknowledge them to God.

Maybe even write down the lies and scribble them out.

Draw Near

Rest in God's presence alongside this person you love. Don't rush it. Just be.

SUBMIT, RESIST, DRAW NEAR—A PRAYER FOR THE WORLD

(For this prayer you will need a map and a candle.)

"Submit yourselves therefore to God. Resist the devil, and he will flee from you. Draw near to God, and he will draw near to you." (James 4:7–8)

Submit the World to God

> Let it all out to God: all the conflict and corruption, the famine and flood, the sickness and war, the evil and sorrow of the world. Surrender this beautiful, broken world to God. Hold open your hands as you pray if it helps you feel a sense of release.

Resist the Accuser

> Now pick a place to pray for. Move your candle there on the map (or if your map is on a screen, place your finger there) and say, "This place, these people, belong to God. Lord, bring your peace."
>
> Pick another place. Move your candle/place your finger there. Say, "This place, these people, belong to God. Lord, bring your peace."
>
> Repeat until you feel complete.

Draw Near to God

> Sit quietly with your hands on the map and listen for what God may want to say to you, or simply sit in God's presence here.

GRATITUDE AND FORGIVENESS— PRAYING FOR THE WORLD

> Take five minutes to brainstorm a list of people—individuals or groups—and write down what comes to you. (This is not people you necessarily need to forgive, or even for whom you are grateful; just list as many different random groups of people you can think of.) They might come to mind from the news, from something

going on in your community or congregation, a global event, relatives, or people you have nothing in common with or even struggle with. Examples include: *kids in foster care, Black Americans, people experiencing homelessness, politicians, people experiencing war, librarians, police officers, farmers, families going through divorce, people who work the night shift, white supremacists, people experiencing violence in the home, people who sort and deliver packages,* really as many and varied as possible.

Pick five individuals or groups from your list that you feel energy around.
They might stir compassion, animosity, distrust, helplessness, sorrow, or admiration.

Write just those five on a separate paper.

Now hold the list of five and invite God to meet you in whatever thoughts or feelings arise in your heart.
Where do you sense gratitude? Name it.
Where are you invited to seek forgiveness? Name it.
Is there pain, anger, or sadness you need to notice and sit with before other invitations can emerge? Name that.

Name the list of five to God a few times, until you sense some love and openness toward the people for whom you are praying.
Sit with that.

Entrust them to God.
Perhaps these five could be lifted in prayer throughout the week.

You may wish to save the list longer list and continue to add to it for future prayer practices. (For example: My congregation has a list of eighty-eight people/groups printed separately on eighty-eight hearts. We've encircled a ten-foot map of the world with the hearts and walked around the circle reading them as a way to pray for the world. We've incorporated them into a weekly morning prayer liturgy of praying for our nation, with a practice of laying some of the hearts with candles on an American flag. We've distributed printable hearts to be cut out and used at home in lots of ways, such as having them in a basket on the kitchen table, pulling out one heart, and naming a person/group every mealtime to pray for during Lent, or choosing three each week to keep in a pocket or on a dashboard or a mirror, to be praying for the needs of others. The possibilities are endless.)

GRATITUDE AND FORGIVENESS—A WALKING PRAYER

Both gratitude and forgiveness begin by accepting what is, right now. It is here that God can meet you.

Walking In
    As you walk into the center, reflect on what is, right now, in your life.
        What are you grateful for?
        What are you not grateful for?
        What are you unwilling to forgive?
        For what do you long for forgiveness?
        What do you long to forgive?

The Center
    Rest in the center with God.

Walking Out
    Walk out with God's Spirit holding you.

After you exit the labyrinth or end the walk, reflect on whatever you want to acknowledge and accept about your life. Write those things down in a journal or on a card. (You could address it to yourself and ask someone to mail it to you in six months.)

PART FIVE

Receiving What Will Be

TWENTY-THREE

Waiting: Living in Anticipation

O n Good Friday, Lake Nokomis Presbyterian Church's Tenebrae ("service of shadows") service ends with Psalm 22 read hauntingly while a bell tolls thirty-three times, once for each year of Jesus's life on earth. Then, in the sorrow and tension, a book is thrown to the ground with a jarring crash, and everyone leaves the darkened church in silence.

For years our family has sought to hold that silence all the way home. It's been a struggle. One memorable year, a mile or two away from church, a loud fart rang out from a car seat, and everyone broke out laughing.

Last year, my kids were seventeen and fourteen. We arrived at the church building at different times. We forgot to have the conversation ahead of time ("Remember, you guys, we go home in silence"). We were scattered in our preferred seats all over the sanctuary for the service. At the end, the lights went down, the bell began tolling, the congregation went quiet and the book crashed to the floor.

People ushered out of the space, without greetings or words, and made their way through the dark hallway to the front door. I went back in the sanctuary with a couple of other folks to unplug microphones and turn off the technology.

When I emerged, my son, who is now eight inches taller than I am, was waiting by the door for me. I touched his arm in thanks, and we headed outside, where my husband and daughter were sitting on the patio. It was then I realized they had picked up the silence and were holding it, inviting me to join them in it.

We silently walked to the car. On the way, two delicious basset hounds, happily bouncing up the sidewalk, their ears practically brushing the ground, came along, a man on the other end of the leash. Maisy and I melted at the sight of them, but the silence held. The ultimate test. I bent down to pat a head, and we nodded to the man and got into our car.

All the way home, the silence held us. Strong and firm. Each one of us committed to it, so each one resting in it. We drove through the city silently. Pausing at stoplights. Passing houses and schools and gas stations on our way to the freeway. The clouds above the skyline were gray on the bottom and soft copper on top. I turned to the back seat to see whether Maisy had noticed them, but she was watching the cars pass by. I turned back toward the clouds and held the silence. It was dark enough to need headlights but barely.

We pulled into the driveway. Doors opened and people got out, but the silence held. We filed up to the door. On the other side of it we could hear our dog standing up on her back legs and pawing at the knob. One of these days she's going to work out how to unlock it and let us in. Andy opened the door and stepped back. She came barreling out, a white blur of wiggling joy, greeting each one of us. I put my face down into her ears. Still we were silent.

When we stepped across the threshold, the spell broke. Immediately there was talk of dinner, a call to remember to hang up coats. Someone began humming as we scattered into the house and on to our own agendas.

This liturgy, the silent drive home on Good Friday, holding within ourselves Jesus's last words as he died, letting it feel heavy and stark, honoring the magnitude and solemnity of it, even just a little bit, by not talking, has taken years of practice. And somehow now, the practice holds us. Even when I forgot it was coming.

Where I live there are very few funeral processions anymore. They used to be so common. The last one I was part of was years ago. A woman who died in her nineties had lived her whole life in our city. As we drove slowly through the city, following the hearse with our flashers on, I was struck by the somberness and beauty of this last drive through the city that was her home. People stopped and watched. The police on motorcycle moved us through red lights and held off traffic. We were holding up the dignity and recognition of a life lived, now over, on this one last pass through the context of that life on the way to a final resting place. She was gone from this city, and we were ushering her out of it and surrendering her to the grave.

This is what the Good Friday silent drive home feels like. Death is getting its due. Now we wait. We enter the vacuum of emptiness that is Holy Saturday. We pause on the other side of death and wait for Easter's release.

As modern people—we don't like to wait. We want to buy what we want when we want it, watch what we want when we want it, go where we want when we want to, do what we want when we want to. We hate to wait in lines or on hold. We don't want to wait; we want to act.

And if we are not acting, we want to be planning. Planning also means not having to endure the discomfort and internal silence of simply waiting. Planning lets us think we can know what to expect and when to expect it. We can soothe our existential terror by either the immediate gratification of action or the imagined control of planning. Either way, we get to draw from our strengths instead of face our weakness. Either way, we get to feel powerful instead of helpless. And either way, we get to avoid the disquiet of waiting.

Both acting and planning have imagination for *what has been*. But waiting, in the Christian sense, cultivates imagination for *what will be.* Christian waiting is anticipating.

When Acts opens, things have been a little weird and intense for the disciples since Jesus was murdered by the state and came back from the dead. Judas has died by suicide. The community has been pretty much in hiding. Then the risen Lord starts popping up places. He's kind of the same but different, both completely familiar and unrecognizable, both available and not. For a little over a month, he's been showing up here and there, walking along with some of them down a road, appearing through locked doors and eating fish, hanging out with them day after day and teaching again like before. And now, he has just literally vanished into the sky before their eyes in what we Christians have come to call the ascension. Jesus has disappeared into the clouds and left the disciples staring up into the sky with their mouths hanging open. They can feel his absence. And yet he promises he will be there with them in a different way, guiding them nonetheless.

So now a new assignment: Jesus said to stay put and wait for the Holy Spirit (Acts 1:4). Whatever *that* means. That's their job, anticipate what they can't imagine. So that's what they are doing. *Constantly devoting themselves to prayer* (Acts 1:14). They're coming together, helping each other learn to trust that God is here now and that God will lead them into what is next.

This is the beginning of this identity: the church is the people who wait. Centuries of Advent have sought to cultivate anticipation in us. Waiting is a calling. We wait for the Holy Spirit to move. We wait for God to act.

But waiting makes us vulnerable and can be excruciating. It's out of our control, and we want control. So maybe the disciples get a little antsy waiting, and they decide to take some action, just a teeny bit. Or at least do some *planning,* so they'll be ready when the time for action comes. They decide they should replace Judas on their leadership team (Acts 1:12–26). And, as they see it, they have two good options before them, Justus and Matthias. Both are followers of Jesus who knew Jesus in the flesh, both men of integrity, both willing to serve. Whom should they choose?

They don't ask themselves WWJD—What would Jesus do, if he were here? Because Jesus is here! Jesus is risen and ascended. We can't see him, we can't touch him, and yet, he is here. Now the community is starting to learn how to live in the paradox of our faith: that Christ is not here but is *here*. They have to look for Christ, learn to be present to the presence of Christ, listen for the voice of Christ, in and through and alongside one another. When we are present with each other, acting with and for one another, Jesus Christ is right here in the space, energy, connection between us. So they're learning to trust this, just like we are.

And then we are given a bizarre and delightful illustration of this blossoming trust. Do they make pro-and-con lists? Debate following Robert's Rules of Order? Launch campaigns and take a vote, the 120 or so of them? No! They draw straws! They flip a coin, roll the dice, "cast lots." They use a game of chance to take things *out* of human hands.

There is nothing intrinsically spiritual or holy about this. We don't think flipping a coin at the beginning of a football game is asking God to choose which team should start. We don't think God is involved when we play rock, paper, scissors over who has to put the kids to bed. Casting lots was just used by the soldiers two months before to divide up Jesus's clothes among themselves while he hung dying on the cross, so it's not like lot casting is some inherently God-seeking process. But when it comes time for the followers of Jesus to pick a leader in witnessing to Christ's resurrection, they roll the dice.

How do we hear God? Sometimes God's voice feels like a quiet little nudge that leads us just the little next step, or the wisdom that sinks into our soul when something in us says, "Yes. That is right." But mostly, we hear God by listening together. By surrendering together. By waiting together. Waiting for the Spirit to direct us. And then acting. And then surrendering and waiting again.

This way of discernment is brazenly different from the world's way—which is fast and decisive. Wayne Muller, in his book *Sabbath*, reminds us,

> The theology of progress forces us to act before we are ready. We speak before we know what to say. We respond before we feel the truth of what we know. In the process, we inadvertently create suffering, heaping imprecision upon inaccuracy, until we are all buried under a mountain of misperception. But Sabbath says, Be still. Stop. There is no rush to get to the end because we are never finished. Take time to rest, and eat, and drink, and be refreshed. And in the gentle rhythm of that refreshment, listen to the sound the heart makes as it speaks the quiet truth of what is needed.[1]

To be in relationship with a living God must begin with trust—that God is real and that God wants to lead us all toward love, toward healing, toward forgiveness, toward righting wrongs, and bringing justice, and birthing hope right in the places of utter despair. It requires that we quiet our souls and wait for God. The church is the people who live honestly in what is and expect God to come. *We wait.* We live in *this* moment, the one given to us *now*. We plan for *this* time, knowing things will change, but not yet knowing how. We don't cling to the past, and we don't

---

1   Wayne Muller, *Sabbath: Restoring the Sacred Rhythm of Rest and Delight* (New York: Bantam Books, 1999), 85.

foreclose on the future. We stay attentive to the movement of the living God by waiting and watching. *What is God doing now? And now? And now? How can we join in right now?*

So maybe God makes the coin flip one way and not the other. God is certainly capable of that. May we too have such trust in God.

Or maybe God thinks it is cute that the eleven are so intent on replacing Judas, as though having twelve disciples—the number Jesus chose when his ministry began, a reflection of the twelve tribes of Israel—is essential for what is to come. As though their structures and systems are vital, their imagination for *what has been* guiding them forward. Of course, they have no idea that just days from now, that wild Holy Spirit will bust the gospel out of its confines and jump-start its spread to the ends of the earth through witnesses who have never seen the human Jesus with their own two eyes, nor heard his voice speaking in a language they wouldn't understand anyway, but who will definitely hear the message their hearts recognize beyond all else and see the risen Lord transform their very souls. The twelve have already become the 120, and in a few days on Pentecost they will become 1,200, and Matthias is never mentioned again in the Bible.

So perhaps when they cast lots, God chooses for them. Or maybe the outcome doesn't matter one way or another to God, but God appreciates their intention just the same. Maybe if they had just waited and skipped the whole exercise altogether, it all would have all turned out the same way anyhow. But God is with them even now as they faithfully seek to do God's will, and that in itself is beautiful and holy. Whether their decision has any effect on things or not, that they would surrender and seek is shaping them all the same.

Their imaginations can't begin to grasp *what will be*, only *what has been*. So they faithfully make their decision.

Then suddenly the whole landscape shifts. And they realize they'd had *no idea* what they'd been waiting for.

The church has always been called to active waiting. It's how we participate in the kingdom of God—which is always breaking in from the future into the present, from the *what will be* into the *what has been*—drawing us to each other, drawing us to God, pulling us out of our settled ruts and our false security, and quieting our souls to watch for the next thing God is doing.

All along the western shores of the islands of Hawaii, vacationers and locals alike assemble in the evening, faces pointed toward the horizon in eager anticipation. I glance down the shoreline, to my left and to my right. Smatterings of people in small groups or alone are leaning against walls, sitting on rocks, gathered on beach chairs, as far down as I can see in either direction.

The show is beginning. Slowly, almost imperceptibly, the sun drops lower in the sky. The clouds shift and colors change, streaks of brilliant yellow, orange, and pink mix like paint with blue to make purple clouds, but it's hard to see it happening unless you are watching closely. Until the very last moment.

The sun takes center stage. After crawling inconspicuously down the sky, the tangerine sun seems to suddenly slide smoothly into its own reflection in the shimmering ocean. The two suns merge until a tiny sliver of brilliant orange remains, and then it is gone. Sometimes there's an audible hum of satisfaction among the watchers. Other times, a smattering of applause.

The people stand, brush off their bottoms, and make their way back to wherever they've come from. The next evening it will happen again. People will come, and they will wait for what they know is coming. They will take in the beauty on purpose, pause to acknowledge the sacredness of the ordinary display of wonder. They will anticipate.

We have a distinct calling in time and place. We are church *for* the world. On behalf of the world, we wait. We watch. We anticipate God's act, and we point out God's in-breaking. *At any moment God might break in and meet us right here.* In hopeful, active anticipation, cultivating imagination for what will be, we wait for encounter with God.

Like those who watch for the sun, we trust it will come and pay attention when it does. We wait for the justice God is bringing and the peace God is bringing. And we wait actively, by living those realities now, even as they are not yet fully here. So we are poised to join in—right now, and right now, and now again—to what God is doing. We don't act for God; we act with God. We know God is coming, is always coming into our death experiences with resurrection and new life. We sit in the places of suffering and despair, of injustice or emptiness, and we wait expectant, attentive, and ready for God together, alongside one another, anticipating redemption.

But unlike the sun-gazers, we let our imaginations be shaped not just for what has been but for what will be. And we hold that promise. With the world. For the world. And when God comes in, in ways we haven't anticipated, we let it shape our future waiting. We keep adapting, keep adjusting, keep responding, keep dying and being born again. We let ourselves be changed, be met, be shaped into the people of God for this time and place. We keep helping each other learn to trust that God is here now, and God will lead us into what is next.

Sometimes too, we are simply stuck in an uncomfortable season of waiting, and it's hard for us to see a way forward. We may be waiting for something that will never come or will not satisfy us when it does. So we need our very waiting to be redeemed by the God who comes in. Christ is with us in these times also, alongside us in the unknown, where we are forced to live so fully in the present because even the next moment may not be clear. We are forced to wait for a way forward to be opened up.

We don't know when or how God might come, might bring redemption in small or big ways to the situations in which we wait. But that is part of the wait too. Entering emptiness, giving death its due, pausing and waiting for Easter's release, letting silence usher us into an awareness shaped by anticipation, we watch, we trust, we hope, we wait, and then we join.

TWENTY-FOUR

Dying: Living without Fear

We are not immortal. This life is not long. We are all dying—some of us are just further along the path than others. We share this journey with each other, no matter where we are along the way.

When Paul wrote 2 Timothy, he was close to death. Old and in prison, Paul was pretty sure he wasn't going to be released. This was his last correspondence with Timothy. This type of writing is called a farewell discourse—a term I find formal and sanitized for such a poignant, personal, painful, and hopeful letter. Paul is saying things he wants Timothy to remember; he is speaking for his own life and his readiness to die, but he is also expressing loneliness and longing to see friends before he goes.

Paul says things like, "When you come, bring the cloak that I left with Carpus at Troas, also the books, and above all the parchments" (4:13). He names those who have done him wrong, expressing forgiveness and letting go of grudges. Passing on greetings, he adds, "Do your best to come before winter" (v. 21) and ends with, "The Lord be with your spirit. Grace be with you" (v. 22).

Paul is dying. He knows he is dying. He acknowledges he is dying and speaks from that place with matter-of-fact boldness, tedious practicalities, and profuse soul-empty-ing. He is tying up loose ends, reaffirming his love and the bonds of relationship, looking back with regret and release, looking ahead with hope, and asking for companionship along the way.

Acknowledging death is part of our faith. When a person is baptized, we paradoxically recognize their life in Christ is beginning with the declaration that this person will one day die. In the very visible action, through water, we give them over to death and receive them resurrected again, risen to a new life in Christ. This is much more visible with the dunking kind of baptism than with a gentle sprinkling. But either way, baptism says we have faced the worst there is and now we have nothing to fear. Our life is in Christ Jesus. Celebrating someone's life with them as they are dying also reminds us all that we have died and risen in Christ. It helps the one who is closer to death remember their baptism and approach death as one who has already faced death and now is held in life—even through and after the passing over from this side of life to the next. It keeps this truth in front of the rest of us as well, so we too may live without fear.

It is said that those who don't fear death are not afraid to live, and we have found this to be true. Our congregation has learned that when one among us is dying, we can look squarely at what is coming and face it together. Whatever we are feeling, we are able to bear it when we share it. Acknowledging a person's dying gives us the chance to tell them what they mean to us. We are able to thank God for their life and let them know we love them. We can find hope together and provide companionship along the way. It makes us brave to live. What more beautiful ministry to each other in all the world is there than this?

The first person who was actively dying whom my congregation formally recognized on that journey was JoAnne. I write about this experience in *The Deepest Belonging* and describe how it opened up space for us to do this again and again.[1] JoAnne had already been doing her own liturgies

---

1   Root, *Deepest Belonging*, 186–93.

toward death, without the rest of the congregation. On a family reunion she had her whole family sign a T-shirt for her as her way of keeping them near to her. She whispered to me after a sermon that she was on her way out of this life. We all knew she was dying; we had been driving her to chemo and knew when she stopped going. But we were not talking about it with each other or with her.

Finally, God jolted me awake to the situation in a dream, and I brought it up with our session (council of elders). "JoAnne is dying, and we are not talking about it." What could we do to honor her and acknowledge this important life moment, this milestone? What could we do to share it with her and not leave her to bear it alone? So with her permission, we designed a gathering we called "A Keeping the Faith Service" based on Paul's words in 2 Timothy 4:7, "I finished the race, I have kept the faith." I told everyone to bring an item that reminded them of JoAnne, and we would share stories about her. With music, words, laughter and tears, silly stories, effusive gratitude, shared memories, a film clip, jars of jam, and handmade mittens, we celebrated JoAnne's life together in the shadow of her impending death.

The Sunday after JoAnne died, the congregation talked together after worship about that service we'd held for her, what it meant to us, what she'd told us it meant to her. And we began to wonder—why don't we talk honestly about what is going on when death is near? The dying person doesn't say anything because they don't want to upset the rest of us. We don't say anything because we don't want to upset them (as though they don't know it's happening). So we all keep silent about a very real—the most real—thing happening to and between us.

But what struck us most about JoAnne's service was that once the ice was broken, once we'd said aloud that this was happening and acknowledged death, the rest of it became very easy. There was no pretending, no holding back. It was easy to laugh, easy to cry, easy to breathe, easy to say the things we would have regretted not having said.

Looking back, we found ourselves wishing we'd talked more openly about her death, and sooner. And looking forward, we wondered whether we could continue to be able to be brave enough to do it again next time. (Spoiler, we were.) We left that experience asking, *How can we be impudent in the face of death?*

After JoAnne, we acknowledged death's approach with several other members. We gathered at Agnes's bedside to sing hymns on her final day. We visited Lois with lemon bars and reminiscences as her time came near. Then the profound experience we had walking through dying with Marty transformed us. It became the impetus for, and through line of, *The Deepest Belonging.*

When Marty stopped his treatment for cancer, we ordained him to a ministry of dying. We recognized Marty's role as a leader among us, as one going before us where we all will one day go. For a year he was honest and real about his experiences and let us share it all with him. When his time came near, he asked for a service like JoAnne's. Only he wanted to be able to actually say goodbye. So that's what we called his service, "Saying Goodbye: An Evening of Storytelling, Gratitude, and Love for Marty."

At Marty's service we strung a clothesline across the front of the sanctuary and printed large sheets of paper that said, "Marty is . . ." and put them with markers on a table at the back of the sanctuary. Marty had invited people from all parts of his eclectic life, and the room filled up with people who answered that question in different ways. We took turns standing and sharing, and pinning our signs to the clothesline. *Marty is brave. Marty is surprising. Marty is mysterious. Marty is hilarious.* The storytelling was sandwiched between a verbal recognition of the great cloud of witnesses Marty would soon be joining and the faithfulness with which he had carried out his ministry of dying among us.

Marty believed most of all that we are all here on earth to help each other, and he lived that out among us. As he sat there that evening, he got to hear us talk about the ways his life had woven in and out of so many other people's lives—how his one, seemingly ordinary life had left a mark on the world. I anointed Marty and told him his baptism would soon be complete, and we finished the evening feasting on his favorite foods in a surprisingly festive goodbye party.

In the services we held for both JoAnne and Marty, once we got past our own existential terror—our own fear of vulnerability and open emotion, our own dread about grief expressed in front of others, our anger at death or worry that once the floodgates opened we would not be able to stem the sorrow—we found on the other side expansive peace. We reached a plane of existing together in a deeply resonant moment, where the presence of God was tangible. Amid the tears was a feeling of indestructible joy. We did not make this happen, didn't even know to long for it. It was given to us. And we received it.

Jen's dying came differently. Fall became winter became spring, and Jen got sicker. Treatment options dwindled and then dried up. The cancer invaded her brain, and quite suddenly her time was shockingly short. Because of hospice visitor limits during the Covid-19 pandemic and also because of Jen's sudden deterioration, no possibility existed for a group gathering with Jen. When Jen's last days approached, I was heading away for a family vacation, and Jen was heading into hospice. I knew I would not be there when she died.

I was able to see Jen in person one last time. She could not speak. Her fragile body was already shutting down. Her spirit was engaged in labor I could not witness.

But I knew she was aware I was there. I held her hand. I told her I loved her, that I honored the hard work she was doing in leaving, and that we'd care for her dear Brian and Ava. She groaned and sighed. I prayed for her, anointed her, and sang Psalm 62, *"My soul finds rest in God alone, my salvation comes from God. My soul finds rest, God is my home,*[2] *I will not be shaken."* I kissed her forehead and said goodbye. That evening I left for Kauai with my family, grateful I had been able to be with Jen before she died.

We arranged a liturgy for Jen's passing. When her time of death was drawing near, Brian would call and let Pastor Lisa know. Lisa would send a message to the congregation, and wherever we were, whatever we were doing, we would all pause. We would stop and hold space for Jen's passing by singing or reciting, *"My soul finds rest in God alone, my salvation comes from God. My soul finds rest, God is my home, I will not be shaken."* It wouldn't need to be long or drawn out, just an intentional choice to stop and be present to what was happening. By honoring her passing wherever we were, each of us would participate in this moment when Jen would escape the bounds of her ravaged body and return to her source of life.

Around 8:00 a.m. the morning after my family arrived in Kauai, we were packing up our supplies to head to a beach. It was 3:00 p.m. at home. The phone rang. Lisa was calling to say Jen's breathing had changed and her time was close.

We made our way to Hideaway Beach and hiked down the slippery, muddy clay trail to the sand below. My family gathered, standing up to our ankles in the ocean, each holding a small piece of washed-up coral. I said, "We don't

2   The song by Sandra McCracken (and the Scripture verse itself) is written with the word *hope*. A typo in our Zoom lyrics early on turned it to *home*. *Home* became the way we continued to sing it on purpose.

know what happens when we die, but we do know we are no longer bound in time and space to our bodies, and Jen is in that space now, on that journey."

I took a breath and continued, "Jen, we love you."

The four of us held silence together, as the water lapped our legs and the clouds gathered overhead. I was keenly aware of all those pausing at this moment all over the world. The church in Minnesota, in their cars or living rooms, or the grocery store, or their backyards. Jen's friends in Milwaukee, Brian's parents in Scotland, my family standing here in the Pacific Ocean. In different time zones and in the midst of different activities, we were united in this task. We were all stopping, as though holding our breath together in holy awe, to honor Jen's journey. All of us, aware, anticipating, paying attention to this thing that was happening, that God was preparing to draw Jen back to her origin and her rest, in limitless, unending love. The Spirit, *ruah* (Hebrew), the breath of God that hovered over the waters at creation and breathed life into the earth creature, the *adam* (Hebrew), now hovered with us all in this suspended pause.

Finally I broke the silence and sang the words, *"My soul finds rest in God alone, my salvation comes from God. My soul finds rest, God is my home, I will not be shaken."* We each released our piece of coral by placing it on a rock or throwing it into the ocean.

It began to rain as we swam and played in the water. A rainbow appeared overhead. The water was choppy; fish were hiding. The rain fell. Water, above, beneath, and all around us. I asked God to show me when Jen passed. A minute later a large fish darted past me, brushing against my legs.

We packed up our things and climbed back up the hill. When we reached the top and cell coverage resumed, I got the message that Jen had died.

From the moment we are born our journey toward death begins. None of us escapes dying. But our life is in

Christ. We've passed through the waters from death to life, and the Holy Spirit hovers over all our living. So just as in baptism, when we sacramentally hand over to death those whose embodied, earthly journey is beginning, in dying, when we finally hand over to death those whose embodied, earthly journeys are ending, they again are passing through the waters from death to life. No loss or sorrow or separation, nothing we've done or left undone, not even death itself, ends life (Rom 8:38–39). Life eternal, which we recognize as love, holds us already and forever in our belonging to God and each other. So, may we not be afraid to live—even the dying part—with and for each other. Then, unabashed, honest, and brave, we will live and we will die, receiving the gift of it all.

TWENTY-FIVE

Hoping: Living the "Even If"

One winter evening when the kids were young, we sat at the family dinner table and lit the first candle in our Advent wreath, the candle for hope. Instead of just reading a little prayer or singing a carol, lighting the candle, and moving on, I asked, "What is 'hope'?"

"What?" Owen asked back, his wheels turning.

And then Maisy chimed in, "I hope for a present."

Andy answered her, "No, Maisy, that's a wish. You wish for a present. Hope is always about wrongs being made right."

"Ohhhh . . . ," said Owen. "Then I hope for no more nightmares."

"And I hope for cancer to be destroyed forever," Andy responded.

"And I hope for peace—for no more wars or fighting ever," I said.

I lit the candle of hope and blew out the match. We all watched the smoke curling toward the ceiling. And then, while we still had the kids' attention, Andy and I talked about how our story comes backwards, from the future to the past. God will make all things right. So God came in to share this life with us in Jesus, and God is with us now in Jesus. That means there is nothing we go through that God does not share. But we live in this in-between time, learning to trust what is coming by sharing where it is breaking in and by noticing where it is not yet. We need to practice trusting, practice waiting and watching for

God. We practice letting the future shape the present and even the past by cooperating with God, as God continues to move even that bad or hard things that have happened toward goodness. Then we read John 1 and talked about the light coming into the world's darkness and darkness never, ever overcoming it.

Advent is for practicing hope. We wait in hope. We live open to being surprised by God. We live aware of those who need kindness. We let ourselves feel the need for things to be made right because we know that one day they will. *We are people of hope*, we told our kids. *Hope is part of who we are.* And by then they were antsy and bored with this installment of dinnertime theologizing, so we stopped talking.

But that Advent changed the ritual of lighting Advent candles for me and also changed my understanding of hope. Hope is paradoxical. The God who is coming is here. The reality that will be is breaking in now. We trust that. David Steindl-Rast calls hope "openness for a future that does not come later." He says, "Some people imagine that hope is the highest degree of optimism, a kind of super-optimism. . . . A far more accurate picture would be that hope happens when the bottom drops out of pessimism. We have nowhere to fall but into the ultimate reality of God's motherly caring."[1] He goes on to say:

> On Easter morning the angel announces the resurrection of Jesus, not by saying, "Here he is; he has come back to life!" No! Looking for him in that way would mean looking for the living one among the dead. He is not here. Nor is he alive with our aliveness that is closer to death than to life. "He is risen" runs the good news, and "He is not here." All we can experience from

---

1   David Steindl-Rast, *Gratefulness: The Heart of Prayer* (Mahwah, NJ: Paulist Press, 1984), 136.

the perspective of our deathbound living is that the tomb is open and empty, a fitting image for wide open hope.

Hope shares the ambiguity of Jesus' cross. Hope is a passion for the possible. . . . And since patience is as contagious as impatience, it will also be our way of strengthening each other's hope.[2]

We don't placate ourselves or others with optimism. We let the bottom drop out of our pessimism. We approach the empty tomb with "perplexed patience," in the midst of our "deathbound living," and let a "wide open hope" take hold in us. We let waiting, patience, and expectation cultivate in us the possibility for what might be and move us toward the future of God breaking in now. We can embody contagious patience. We can strengthen one another and affect the world around us by practicing contagious patience together. We can let it lead us toward hope.

Advent, the season of waiting in perplexed and contagious patience for Christ's coming, is a bold and prophetic act. By lighting a candle for hope, we name the things we wait for, we say they are coming, and we declare that even now we see and feel them and assert they are real. And if we're brave, we also name the things we wait in—our fears, our battles, our struggles and sadnesses—and so say these things too belong to God and *we* belong to God as we wait.

We open ourselves to hope this way again in Lent. We don't typically think of Lent as a hopeful season, but it is. Lent invites us to face our fear full-on, to look at our terror and the way the threats of failure, loss, and death direct our lives. Fear paralyzes us. It is loud, and looming, and we give it the mic because it's demanding and authoritative. Fear can make hope seem shallow and silly and ungrounded.

2 Steindl-Rast, *Gratefulness*, 160.

We start to hope, and immediately fear roars up behind us, listing all the things that could go wrong.

But hope is stronger than fear. Fear is temporary and temporal. It comes from the stories we tell ourselves about what might happen. We imagine bad things, we dread loss, we see what's coming and believe it will overwhelm and defeat us. *What if . . . what if . . . what if . . .* fear whispers. Then it shifts to the threat: *What if . . . I won't be safe. I won't have enough. I won't belong. I won't be seen. I'll lose someone I love, lose my security, my comfort, my place.* Worry rehearses fear's lies, over and over again; it whispers that we are unsafe, abandoned, futureless, and ultimately alone. In other words, fear tells us we don't belong to God and we don't belong to each other.

But hope's response to "what if . . ." isn't optimism's "That will never happen!" Hope doesn't say, "Cheer up!" "That's not true!" or "It's not as bad as you think!" Hope's response to fear is "Even if . . ." *Even if* the very worst thing that could happen does happen, it will still be OK. *Even if*, as the psalmist says, *the mountains fall into the heart of the sea* (Ps 46:2), that is *still* not the biggest thing. God is still God. Love is still the first and truest and final word. "God is our refuge and strength, a very present help in trouble. Therefore I will not fear" (vv. 1–2), because we belong to God and we belong to each other. No matter what! And, as many theologians, writers, and musicians[3] have noted, *if it is not OK, then it is not the end.*

Fear is finite, but hope is infinite. Hope comes from outside us, reaches from before us, and stretches out beyond us. Hope helps us exist inside the promise from the Divine about a future we can't create. Grounded firmly in reality, hope tells the truth both of what we're facing *and* of the

---

3   Ferdnando Sabino, Paulo Coelho, Frederick Buechner, John Lennon, and Sandra McCracken, among many others.

bigger picture. Hope is the heart that keeps on beating, *Even if . . . even if . . . even if . . .*

So to turn toward hope, we need to embrace the experiences we are in—even the fear. We need to be willing to look at our sin—which is just a fancy word for our disconnection from God and each other in all the many ways that plays out. We need to tell the truth about the brokenness, the malice, and the evil, inside us and around us. Hope is *always* about wrongs being made right. So we need to look wrong in the face and call it wrong. And this is what Lent invites us to do.

In Lent we notice our own brokenness and the brokenness in the world around us. We let ourselves feel it and grieve it, and we say boldly, *Things are not as they should be!* because we know there is more; we know this is not the end. We let the bottom drop out of our pessimism and we fall into God's motherly care. Hope is knowing it could be different, it *should* be different, it *will* be different.

Jesus came into all of it, the fear of it, too—his weakness and temptation in the wilderness, his terrible grief at the loss of his friend Lazarus, his all-consuming dread in the garden anticipating his own death. Jesus did not back down from the fear. Because he was without sin, because he lived completely in his belonging to God and each other, he could go into the fear and grief and loss and stay connected to God. He could reach through the fear to the hope.

We are the body of Christ. We are the people of hope. And so we are people who do not cower from fear and are not afraid to hope. We let God pull us through the finite fear to the hope that is infinite. One day, despite all we see and hear and feel, love triumphs, life prevails. Peace reigns. Justice rules. The weak are made strong. All that has been lost is restored. This is God's promise. The love of God is "vast, unmeasured, boundless, free."[4] This is our hope. And so, in Advent's waiting, in Lent's honesty, and with the contagious patience of those who know the tomb is open and empty, we live toward "a future that doesn't come later." We hope.

---

4   From the hymn "O the Deep, Deep Love of Jesus" by S. Trevor Francis, 1873.

TWENTY-SIX

Imagining: Living Now
What Will Be

S everal years ago, I was part of creating a new vision
statement for our presbytery that caused a bit of hoopla
when it was debuted. Ready to hear the controversial statement? "We fearlessly follow the Holy Spirit into a changing
world." Guess which word caused so much anxiety for people on every end of every conceivable spectrum? *Fearlessly.*

We sometimes act as though anxiety equals faith. We
would never say this, but we behave as though worrying
and fretting over situations means we *care*, and that continuing to care shows we are faithful. Or we think faith
needs some humility attached to it, some good, old-fash-
ioned fear mixed in to keep us in check. Whatever the
reason, *fearlessly* made some people fearful. Perhaps it's
the audacity of the word. It is a reckless word, daring and
caution throwing. *Fearlessly.* Shamelessly. Brazenly. Take
your pick. Also, it's a word that holds our feet to the fire.
It's no halfway word. It's an all-out, no-holds-barred word.
Fearless.

But the visioning team chose the word deliberately. It
is a future word. It is the word most spoken (365 times in
scripture!) by messengers of God from creation to revelation
and everywhere in between: *Fear not, do not be afraid. I
come from the new, where hope is realized and God's promises
are fulfilled, and I speak to you from God. Do not be afraid,
for God is doing something new. For God is with you. For*

God is leading you. For all these things around you that seem so big and scary and overwhelming, these things do not have the ultimate power over you. God does. Fearlessly follow.

But we're not very good at fearless (or following, for that matter). We're not very good at living out of the future. We'd rather use the knowledge of the past to manage the risks of the present and behavior-modify ourselves into God's kingdom. We can be good, ethical, or "on the right side of history." We can love our neighbor—or at least strive to—if that's what makes God happy. We can feed the hungry, at least when they're on our radar screen, because we know it's the right thing to do. But what kind of dangerous, wild, and unruly territory are you suggesting we enter when you say that we'll fearlessly follow the Holy Spirit into a changing world? We're quite comfortable with timidly inviting the Holy Spirit into our dormant churches, and even that feels a tad risky.[1]

But the people of God, who live in the Way of God, the kingdom of God, are people with "eschatological imagination." *Eschatological* has to do with "the very, very end." And *imagine* means "to form new ideas, or images, or concepts of external objects not present to the senses."[2] We let the concepts and images of God's future bend back to shape our present. We live now from what is coming.

When my son, Owen, was in kindergarten, he was having trouble with someone teasing him. The boy was relentless, and Owen was getting more and more frustrated and filled with despair. He would have to talk to the boy.

In the end, what empowered him to speak to the other kid (when he really wanted to punish him), what helped

---

1   After an intensive group process a decade ago developing the presbytery's vision statement including a lively public discussion at its debut and many years of displaying it, I was surprised to discover just recently that the word *fearlessly* has, mysteriously and quietly, disappeared from our vision statement. It is simply no longer there.

2   *Oxford English Dictionary*, s.v. "imagine."

him to reach out and respectfully engage the boy, was not some idea that he "should" do that because good kids, or Christian kids, or whatever, are nice and not mean. Believe it or not, what empowered Owen was his eschatological imagination. He was able to envision a reality where everybody could be strong without making other people weak, to imagine it so fully that he could live from it without even seeing it in front of him.

What he had been experiencing was a kid finding strength by making him weak. And his wounded and justice-seeking self wanted to be bigger and make that boy tiny enough to squash him! He imagined that story line for a while. But when he wrestled through the pain of the experience, and with help began to see how that feeling of weakness made him long for strength the same way this little boy might be longing for strength too, it fired up Owen's eschatological imagination, and the child could not go to sleep. For over two hours, he called me into his room every time had a new idea, something he would say to the kid, some way he would reach out.

He got so grounded in this reality, in this identity, that he began to say that he was someone with kindness inside, someone who could be strong and help others feel strong. He owned that identity, stepped into it, and tried it on until it felt comfortable. He went to school—utterly undaunted by a smart-ass kid we passed on our way in who made a comment to him (while it was all I could do to keep from grabbing *that* kid's cheeks in my hands and giving him a good come-to-Jesus right then and there!).

But Owen, unfazed, was living from a new reality, a future reality that was not yet realized, where people didn't have to make others feel weak in order to be strong. He didn't have to make others feel weak, and that identity made him strong. Somehow, he got up the nerve to respectfully ask the child to please stop doing what he had been doing to Owen. And a few days later, he reported with a huge smile that the boy had asked Owen if he could be friends with him.

This is kindergarten conflict we're talking about here. But I hid the tears in my eyes when his teacher said in the conference at the end of the month, "Owen treats his classmates with respect and kindness. He solves conflicts in peaceful ways." Because I had seen the struggle it had taken him to get in touch with his eschatological imagination and live from that place. And because watching him do it gave me hope.

We don't treat others with respect and kindness because that is what we're *supposed* to do. We don't do it because we really, truly believe that our kindness will spread and one day wipe out all disrespect. We don't stand up for justice because we think we can end injustice or because the Bible says so. We do these things because as people of faith we bend our lives toward the reality that is not yet fully here, because we live into the coming of God—when there will be no injustice, or unkindness, when all people's dignity and humanity will be upheld.

The church is not the place where people go to be good, or learn how to be good, or ease their guilt for not being good. And it's not meant to be where we timidly sing our hymns and anxiously pray our prayers and fearfully strive to please God without asking too many hard questions or getting weighed down by life's difficulty. No. The church is the people who we audaciously live out now what is coming, who fearlessly practice it even if we don't yet see it. We fire up our eschatological imaginations together and live from the shared awareness of what is coming.

We give to the poor not because we think we can eliminate poverty or because we are obligated to do so by our religion (Luke 12:33–34). We share what we have with those who have less because we have the eschatological imagination to envision the day when there will be no more rich or poor and everyone will have enough. So we witness to that day by living it out now. We neither cause nor prevent God's kingdom from coming; we participate in the kingdom of God unfolding among us. We join in what God is already doing.

We worship not because we think God needs it or it makes us good people. We turn our hearts together to our Source because the day is coming when God will be so close to us that we will delight in God's presence and God will delight in us, when we'll barely open our mouths and God will hear our needs and respond, when there will be no more weeping or despair or sadness, only closeness and belonging and fulfillment.

Practicing what will be, singing and praying and living the future into view, this is active hope. Hoping is trusting that God is bringing God's future, and bending our lives, our wills, our imaginations toward that future. It is letting the possibility of it fill us so completely that it guides us more than the problems we see around us.

And because it is eschatological, it is always becoming, never complete, and also found right here, already begun. Our eschatological imagination fuels the way we live our lives. It alerts us deep in our core to the places in the world where the things of God's promised future are lacking, and when it does, we live from their fulfillment, even when we can't yet see it completely. We live in honesty and wholeness and peace; we practice kindness and respect; we work for justice and equity—because this is the shape of God's future. So, as disciples of Jesus Christ, we live that future out now before it is here in its fullness, in *anticipation of* and *participation in* the coming kingdom of God. We know where this is going, and we see our place within it. This makes us kind, hopeful, and brave.

The writers of our Scriptures had eschatological imagination. They premembered all the time. In Isaiah 65:17–25, the prophet says, "For I am about to create new heavens and a new earth; the former things shall not be remembered or come to mind. But be glad and rejoice forever in what I am creating; for I am about to create Jerusalem as a joy, and its people as a delight." Then he goes on to list all the specific characteristics of this new reality God is promising: no more weeping or cries of distress, no more infants living a few days or old people's lives cut short. Those who build houses get to live in them, they'll plant vineyards and be around long enough to enjoy the fruit from them, they'll plant fields and nobody will pillage them. "They shall not labor in vain, or bear children for calamity; for they shall be offspring blessed by the LORD—and their descendants as well. Before they call I will answer, while they are yet speaking I will hear" (vv. 23–24). Violence will end; no longer will animals be divided into predator and prey; they will eat and sleep alongside each other. And "'They shall not hurt or destroy on all my holy mountain,' says the LORD" (v. 25).

Martin Luther King Jr.'s "I Have a Dream" speech was an exercise in eschatological imagination. In this speech he honestly names aloud the failure of America to live up to its promise and potential, its "sacred obligation" to all its citizens. He calls out the injustice, discrimination, poverty, and violence toward Black Americans, and declares that the cry for equality will not be appeased or silenced until "justice rolls down like waters, and righteousness like a mighty stream" (Amos 5:21–23).

Then, using the imaginative language of a dream, King describes his eschatological vision, painting a vivid picture of what the future of God breaking into America looks like. The descendants of slaves and descendants of slave owners dining together at the table of belonging, the glaring injustice of Mississippi becoming instead a shining light of justice for the whole nation to follow.

On and on, using his eschatological imagination, he vibrantly illustrates true freedom for all. Quoting the eschatological vision of the Prophet Isaiah (40:4–5), he thunders,

RECEIVING WHAT WILL BE

"Every valley shall be lifted up, and every mountain and hill be made low; the uneven ground shall become level, and the rough places a plain. Then the glory of the Lord shall be revealed, and all people shall see it together!"

Then King names hope—right out of despair, hope with the power to transform chaos to beauty—to be what guides, inspires, and directs all those fighting for justice and standing up for freedom. Hope is what binds them together and propels them forward as they pray, and march, and face adversity. Martin Luther King Jr's trust that God is leading all things toward freedom is what grounded him, and he sought to infuse courage into people to let what *will be* shape what *is*. (If it's been a while since you last heard it, I invite you to read or listen online, and hear MLK's eschatological imagination sing forth in his own voice).

Eschatological vision invites deep honesty and fearless imagination. It first invites us to consider, What godforsakenness, grief, or yearning do you bear? Where is there brokenness and stuckness in your life or in the world? Then it prompts you to imagine, How does God's future meet you in those places?

If I activate my eschatological imagination, I can envision a day when all people will recognize one another as siblings, beyond fear, past judgment, and each person will feel seen, known, and understood. And that can help me move into my day seeing people with compassion and kindness. It can make me speak up and persist toward connection even when it feels terrifying.

One day we will all value and tend to the earth and its creatures, living in harmony within nature, letting creativity and wonder and deep appreciation for the cycles of life and living guide us in loving the land and sea and sky. So I can right now let my daughter teach me about microorganisms and learn together how to grow vegetables and compost our table scraps. I can let her persuade us to get chickens, whom I have utterly fallen in love with. I can take joy in feeding birds and buy fresh veggies from my local CSA (community supported agriculture) and donate to the Environmental Defense Fund. I can share a single car with the other three drivers in my family and take buses, or walk, or bike when we can. None of these small acts is saving the world, but all of them are faithfully joining in the salvation God is already and always bringing. And they help us live now what will be.

In the very, very end there will be no cancer. No surprise new viruses demanding vigilant caution. No fear of disease or diagnoses. Life will be free of worry about ADHD or IQ or SATs or STDs or the million other accidents, injuries, injustices, disabilities, and disorders that threaten our children. So right now I can let love guide me through that next doctor's appointment, school screening, or heartbreaking phone call from a friend. I can call up a sick relative and check in. I can face the next crisis with courage. I know where all this is heading. I know that all the things our world says have the power to hinder or destroy us do not have the final say. So in any scary or worrisome circumstance, I can trust that God's fullness and life meets us *even if,* and I can be a conduit of that love and life.

I want to be a person with a rich eschatological imagination, whose capacity for envisioning what is coming is extravagant and robust, fueled by hope. I want my now to be directed by God's future. God is bringing peace, healing, and wholeness, and moving everything toward this end. Because the resurrection is real, love is stronger than fear, Jesus has conquered death, and the conclusion of all things being made new is impending,[3] I can receive this life now. We can participate now in what will be. We can fearlessly follow the Holy Spirit into a changing world.

3   I'm grateful to Rev. Jess Harris Daum for this wording.

TWENTY-SEVEN

Prayers for Receiving What Will Be

MEET US IN THE WAITING—A PRAYER OF HOPE

God, who meets us now,
meet me now.
Help me wait for you to meet me here.
Help me watch for how you meet me.

God who loves us now,
love us now.
Help me wait for your love to come.
Help me watch for how your love comes.

God who heals us now,
heal us now.
Help me wait for you to heal us.
Help me watch for how your healing comes.

God whose future meets us now,
meet us with your future now.
Help me wait for your newness to break in.

In the places of death,
help me watch for your new life.
In the places of division,
help me join in your work of love.
In the tension of unrest,
help me trust in your reality of peace.
Amid the disappointment, anxiety, and vulnerability
within and around me,
infuse me with your hope,
that I may bear hope in the world.
Amen.

REDEEM MY WAITING—A PRAYER

God, the waiting is so hard.
What am I waiting for, really?
I think I am waiting for . . .
    (Name the things.)
because I am telling myself . . .
    *(Name the stories you are telling yourself about
    why you are waiting.)*

God, help me wait for you.
Help me watch for you.
Help me sense your presence.
Help me follow your guidance.
Help me join in your kingdom, breaking in now,
all around me, moving the whole story,
toward life and fullness.
Teach me to wait.
Make me someone who waits,
hopeful and brave.
Amen.

FOLLOW, SEEK, BREATHE—A
PRAYER OF REORIENTATION

Follow me, Jesus says.
Yes, we answer.
But how to follow?
What to do or not do?
What to learn or unlearn?
What to say or not say?
What to read or not read?
What to eat or not eat?
How to think or not think?
What to believe or not believe?

Seek me first, Jesus says.
Yes, we answer.
But how to seek?
What to look for or look at?
What to listen to or listen for?
What to cling to or let go?
What to take up or put down?
What to fight for or against?

We hear so many voices,
with so many answers
to so many questions.
Which ones are right?
How do we know?

Breathe.
Again.
Now.
Open your eyes.
Look.

Open your ears.
Listen.

Jesus is here.
God is near.
About to act in any moment.

Watch for it.
Wait for it.
You will know when you see.
You will recognize when you hear.

The Spirit of God will
shape you

into a disciple.
One little step after the last.

You will see deeper,
you will listen wider,
you will recognize quicker,
you will join in sooner.
You will seek and you will follow.
God will do this.
Changing hearts and lives is what God does.
You simply say, Yes
and begin.

CONTAGIOUS PATIENCE—A PRAYER FOR HOPE

God of all times and beyond all time,
cultivate in me openness for your
future that doesn't come later.
Give me honesty, even unto pessimism.
Hold me in your motherly care.

Bring us through death to real aliveness.
Teach me to recognize real aliveness;
let me be seized by passion for what is possible.

Give me contagious patience
to wait for hope.
May a wide-open hope meet me,
O Lord, I wait.
Amen.

TWENTY-EIGHT

Practices for Receiving
What Will Be

FROM FEAR TO TRUST—PRAYING FOR OTHERS

May be done verbally or through writing.

Worry is practicing fear. Rest is practicing trust. Most of the time when we think we are praying for someone else, we are just shooting our worrying in God's direction. What would it look like to get through the fear to the trust?

First, recognize the fear.
"Plea dumping" is intentionally pouring out all our stuff to God—anxiety, longing, terror, ruminations, anger, sorrow, projections. Say it all, beg, yell, argue, whatever needs to come. Be honest and dump it all out.

Then let yourself listen to God.
Be with God in the space on the other side of the venting, where there is likely grief that needs releasing. Let yourself go there. Let yourself collapse like a scared and sad child into the arms of God.

Then you can turn to interceding from a place of trust instead of fear.
Pray these or similar words.
God, help me trust you with _____.
Help me see you at work in _____.

CULTIVATING AN ESCHATOLOGICAL IMAGINATION—A JOURNALING PROMPT

What are the places of deepest sadness and longing in you?
Maybe it's a specific situation, relationship, circumstance. Or maybe it's broader. What brokenness in

the world most calls to you? Sit and let yourself feel
the sorrow, fear, anxiety, and worry.
If you wish, write it down.

What would complete wholeness look like?
What is the life you long for most in this circumstance, situation, or relationship? *The fullness of flour-
ishing would be . . .*
Write your eschatological vision of God's future.

Now imagine yourself walking in that reality, sharing
now in what will be.
What actions can you take in this situation that
would ground you in the Way of God instead of
the Way of Fear? How can you participate in God's
redemption in this circumstance?
Write the invitations you sense.

PRAYING FOR LOVED ONES IN SUFFERING

Praying for others sometimes feels like worrying with the
words, "Please, God, . . ." at the beginning. It does not feel
like fullness or life; more often it's anxiety and anguish.

This time when you pray for your person, try holding all
three of these truths in you at the same time:

1. You cannot do anything to change the situation of the
   person you love.
   This truth is painful and difficult.
2. God is able to do anything.
   It doesn't hurt to ask for what you really want.
3. No matter what, God's salvation, healing, and love can
   meet us in and work within our lives as they are.

Even if our circumstances at the moment are terrible, even in the midst of something awful, God's fullness and life are possible for the other person and for you.

ADVENT CANDLE LIGHTING LITURGY

The word *Advent* means "coming." In this season counting down to Christmas, we celebrate God's coming to us in Jesus's birth at Christmas; we celebrate that Christ is with us now and wait for Christ's return. Advent is a time of waiting, and hoping, and trusting in the God who was, and is, and is to come. *In this liturgy the words spoken together are in bold.*

Advent 1: Candle of Hope
(purple/blue candle)
> In the beginning was the Word,
> and the Word was with God,
> and the Word was God.
> The light shines in the darkness,
> and the darkness did not overcome it.
> The Word has come to live among us.
> **We wait for the light of Christ.**
> **Today we light a candle for HOPE.**
> > *(Hope candle is lit.)*

> Dear God,
> As we begin our Advent waiting, we pray for hope.
> **Give us the courage to hope.**
> **Hope that we are not alone,**
> **hope that this is not the end,**
> **hope that you are always with us now and you**
> **promise you always will be.**
> *(Sing one verse of "O Come, O Come, Emmanuel.")*

Advent 2: Candle of Peace
(purple/blue candle)

> In the beginning was the Word,
> and the Word was with God,
> and the Word was God.
> The light shines in the darkness,
> and the darkness did not overcome it.
> The Word has come to live among us.
> **We wait for the light of Christ.**

> Last week we lit a candle for HOPE.
> > *(Hope candle is lit)*
> **Today we light a candle for PEACE.**
> > *(Peace candle is lit)*

> Dear God,
> In our Advent waiting, we pray for PEACE.
> **Give us the courage to seek peace.**
> **peace in our hearts,**
> **peace in our relationships with others,**
> **peace in the places we live, and peace in all the**
> > **world.**
> *(Sing one verse of "O Come, O Come, Emmanuel")*

Advent 3: Candle of Joy
(pink candle)

> In the beginning was the Word,
> and the Word was with God,
> and the Word was God.
> The light shines in the darkness,
> and the darkness did not overcome it.
> The Word has come to live among us.
> **We wait for the light of Christ.**

The first week of Advent, we lit a candle for HOPE.
> *(Hope candle is lit)*

The second week of Advent, we lit a candle for PEACE.
> *(Peace candle is lit)*

Today we light a candle for JOY.
> *(Joy candle is lit)*

Dear God,
In the depth of our Advent waiting we pray for joy.
Give us the courage to experience joy.
Joy in the face of scary things,
joy in the face of sad things,
joy in the face of unknown things.
> *(Sing one verse of "O Come, O Come, Emmanuel")*

Advent 4: Candle of Love
(purple/blue candle)

In the beginning was the Word,
and the Word was with God,
and the Word was God.
The light shines in the darkness,
and the darkness did not overcome it.
The Word has come to live among us.
We wait for the light of Christ.

The first week of Advent, we lit a candle for HOPE.
> *(Hope candle is lit)*

The second week of Advent, we lit a candle for PEACE.
> *(Peace candle is lit)*

The third week of Advent, we lit a candle for JOY.
> *(Joy candle is lit)*

Today we light a candle for LOVE.
> *(Love candle is lit)*

Dear God,
As our waiting comes to its end, we pray for love.
Give us the courage to welcome your love.
To know the love you have for each of us,
to share the love you have for the people it is hard
to love,
and to see your love all around us.

On Christmas Eve we will light the candle of Christ
in the center of the wreath
because in Jesus,
hope, peace, joy, and love are brought to life
and made to live in us.
Christ is the light of the world!
(Sing one verse of "O Come, O Come,
Emmanuel.")

REMEMBERING THE REAL—A PRAYER FOR THE WORLD

All people belong to God, and all people belong to each
other, everywhere, always, and that will be the final
word over the whole earth. When we remember this,
we are free.

Before you pray, imagine the whole world remembering, all
at once.

Imagine each place, filled with people remembering we
belong to God and each other.

Remembering our own holiness and the holiness of
each other.
Remembering it is only love that remains.

Remembering that there is actually nothing to compete for; there is already enough.

Imagine what would happen between people, between nations . . . imagine villages and neighborhoods, towns and cities, where everyone trusts this belonging with their whole being.

Imagine everyone, everywhere, living in this freedom, this belonging, this remembering.
Let yourself spend time imagining this.

When self-judgment or corrective voices arise to tell you statistics and struggles and messages of hopelessness, gently welcome them by saying, "Oh! Look how fearful it is to imagine complete freedom! Thank you for your service. You may go now." And return to your imagining.

When you are finished imagining the world as God intended it to be, pray for the world however you feel led.

PART SIX

Receiving This Life

TWENTY-NINE

Sing: A Charge for Receiving This Life

B*ased on Psalm 98*

Sing a new song. Try it. Something completely new. Something you've never sung before. You don't know the words, you can barely hum the tune, but sing it anyway.

Try it on for size . . . no, just jump in and belt it out. Maybe you don't sing with the confidence you would if it were the old song, the familiar song, the song that makes sense and feels easy. Maybe you don't feel so comfortable with the instruments, or you worry that you'll be singing alone.

Tell you what—how about if we sing with you?

And not just us, the whole earth—the chaotic seas will sing too, and they can't sound more in tune than you do—the floods will clap their messy hands; just make a joyful noise, really, any noise will do.

But make it loud, OK?

Because the hills are going to join in on this, and actually, the world itself, and all those who live in it. It will be a song like no other, so get ready to sing.

Are you ready?

This song, it means something.

This is one reason it is a new song and not the old
songs. It is not a song of proper religion. It is not
a song of patriotism or a song of war. It is not a
lament for how terrible things are or a song of
social consciousness or commentary.

This song simply can't be sung by "us and them," or
played on bandwagons or soapboxes, and it's not
a rally song, a commercial jingle, or background
music in an elevator. It's not like the old songs in
any way at all, so you need to let all those go if
you're really going to sing this song.

This is also not a lullaby we'll be singing here; this
song is more of a wake-up-and-take-notice type
song. It is a remember-and-never-ever-ever-forget
kind of song.

It is a song for all the times when you were treated
unfairly, and not only you, but all those who
were treated unfairly, ever—even by you. It is
a song for the times you were overlooked and
undervalued, the times you were nothing but
a number, or a diagnosis, or an accessory, or a
liability.

This is a song for the ravaged and destroyed creation;
over the parched, burning, and starving earth,
it sings crashing seas and clapping floods and
quenching rain. And where she's drowning in
sorrow, it lifts the ground from waterlogged
sludge and drapes it gently over the line to dry in
the tender breeze and warm sun. It's *that* versa-
tile and powerful a song.

This is a song for all the times when evil won, and
those times were many and great—countless, or

so we thought—it sings right in the face of those
times, it thrusts its wide eyes and unquenchable
joy right up under the nose of those times and
opens its mouth and belts out with all gusto
right into the shocked and startled face of evil,
knocking it down on its bottom to stare up in
stunned standstill at the wild and mighty sound
of the song.

This is a song of justice that tears through the
paper-thin fragility of justice and liberty for
all, that lifts up all the incidences—*every single
one*—where injustice and oppression were really
the rule, where lives didn't matter as much as
money, where people were forsaken for power—
the song, you will hear it, has every one of their
voices, loud and strong, vindicated and joyful.
Each forsaken child, every cheated worker, and every
single starving, sick, disregarded, or devalued
human being that has ever been, all the silenced
and ignored and unheeded voices, will rise
together in a sound so great that it shatters glass
ceilings into a million pieces, reduces palaces to
rubble, and grinds diamonds to dust. A sound so
powerful it drowns out every bomb and bullet
and lie and label, and quakes open the prisons
and graves and sets the captives free. So get
ready, because this is *some* song.
This is not just any song; it is the song of the earth
for her king, her Creator; this is a song of all
things made right.

But you know, this song, actually, is kind of a dangerous song.
It is not a song for the faint of heart. We already
discovered you don't need to really know the

words, or even the tune; you don't have to have
practiced or learned this song; in fact, there is
really no way to do so, you just sing it.
But you have to be willing to sing it.
Are you willing to sing it?
Because if you hear this song you can't ever go back.
You can't pretend you didn't hear it. You can't be the
way you were before you sang it.
It changes you, but not just you; it changes
everything.
So, if you're comfortable with how things are, I
mean, if you don't really want to see things too
terribly different, then you'd better not sing the
song.
Just to be safe.
Because there are no secrets once this song has been
sung.
There is nothing hidden that doesn't get revealed.
And all the things that look strong, or sure, or
important, they might seem kind of silly and
stupid once you hear this song. So, if you care a
whole lot about those things, better not to sing
it, at least not just yet. Let them get tarnished
first, broken in, disappointing. Let the expectations get a little bit dashed and the frustration
build a bit, because this song is for everyone
and everything, except it is NOT a song for the
satisfied.
It is not a song for the secure and the worthy, for the
strong and the powerful, and it certainly doesn't
make you right or tell you who's wrong. It kind
of makes a joke of all that.
So if that is where you're at, better to cover your ears
and turn away for as long as you can stand it
before it overpowers you, because you're going

to be really cut down to size, and I can't imagine
that will be a very pleasant experience.

But once you are, there is a place for you in this song
too.
Actually, that's kind of the only way you can join
in the song, when you know that in singing it,
you pass judgment on yourself, but you sing it
anyway.
Because—and this is the most important part,
maybe I forgot to say this—the song is not about
you. It's actually not really about any of us, or
anything we know or have done or ever will do.
It's about God.
It's all about God.
It's about what God has done and what God will do.
It's about God, who *does* things and doesn't just
watch it all and keep to Godself.
But God watches too, and doesn't miss a thing either,
so there is nothing, *nothing* that doesn't get
made right in this song.

It sounds like kind of a lot, and it is, actually.
It's everything.
Way more than you or I could ever bear. Way more
joy and justice than we would know what to do
with in a thousand lifetimes.

But we don't really need to worry about it. We just
need to pay attention. The chorus is coming.
And when you're paying attention, you get to see
that it has already started. Here and there it star-
tles you, or makes you cry for no reason, or gives
you a weird thrill of recognition and irrational
hope.

We've found ways to explain it away, the crazies, the anomalies, the exceptions, the sentimental or insane, but they're not, really, they're the song, peeking through the frayed seams, busting through a rip in the knee or a tear in a button-hole of the fabric of our so-called reality.

The stranger stands and shouts a few notes before helping someone off the bus. The man on the overpass with the sign grips the change in his fist and hollers a bit of the melody into the pass-ing traffic below. Neighbors lying side by side through the night echo defiant snippets through train tunnels—the tune bounces off the walls and wraps around the sleeping grandmothers and shopkeepers, while bombs drop overhead. Our own winter-weary bodies vibrate with the symphony of the overjoyed spring soil as we plunge our hands into the teeming universe below and turn our spent souls upward toward the sun.

In fact, all over the world, if we just know how to listen, above us, beneath us, before us, and afterwards, too, we'll hear that the song has begun; and the very earth itself is humming in anticipation.

Just lift your gaze to the drifting clouds and breathe, or tune your ears to the skittering, chirping creature commotion. Close down the computer, shut off the phone, turn off the TV and the lights, and curl up at an open window as the day slips into night and crickets and katydids hold a steady chorus beneath the city sounds.

The noise is building.

And we, you and I, together, we sing the song. It's what we do.

It's why in the world we get together and do this
thing called worship that accomplishes nothing
at all, as any reasonable person familiar with the
old songs could tell you.
We come together to share song, to remember the
truth, to recount the steadfast love of our Lord,
the coming and sharing and dying and rising,
backwards and upside down, breaking in and
spilling out, never-ending and always-persisting
salvation of our God-with-us.
We warm up our voices and pipe out a few notes
in defiance of the deafening silence, in far-
fetched musical mutiny to the grating discord
of the world around us, and really, on its behalf,
because like it or not, ready or not, the song is
coming.
So we might as well sing along.

THIRTY

Receive: A Benediction

F*or You, Dear Reader*
Beloved child of God, receive this benediction:

May you know yourself to be held in God's love.
May you know this whole world to be held in God's
love.
May you see each person you encounter this week as
held in God's love.
No matter what and always,
the world belongs to God.

May you trust this.
And when you forget,
may you be still and let God show you.

May you live alongside others,
confessing brokenness,
embracing forgiveness,
upholding each other in weakness,
and bearing death together.

May you watch for God's surprises,
share stories of resurrection,
abide in Christ's love,
and wait for the Spirit to lead us to what is next,
and when that happens,
may you act.

May you sing the brave song,
and from time to time, stop,
be silent,
and bear witness to the wonder of this life.

May you bless this weary world,
and your fellow travelers here.

May you bless, and bless, and bless.

May you sense God's delight in you,
and with joy,
may you receive this life.
Amen.

Acknowledgments

I am grateful for Lake Nokomis Presbyterian Church. Thanks for watching for God and practicing the deepest belonging with me. Your boundless imagination and tenacious longing to notice God and join in Christ's ministry invites good liturgy. Thank you to Erin DeBoer-Moran, LNPC's director of music and worship arts, for your collaboration, creativity, attunement to the Holy Spirit and people, and your desire to always cram in as much and varied music as possible. I am grateful for my editor, Beth Gaede, who helped me sort, shape, and simplify what began as a daunting, confused pile of material; you are a master. Thank you to Rev. Lisa Larges and Rev. Phil GebbenGreen for attempting to read this manuscript while it was still a jumbled word salad and hanging in with me as it took form. I so appreciate your honesty, friendship, and partnership in ministry.

Thank you to Rev. Dr. Theresa Latini, for our weekly "writing days," squirreling ourselves away in the basement of the retreat center, keeping each other on task and in tune. Your companionship and mutual commitment to that invaluable routine gave this manuscript the concentrated space it needed to come to life.

Thank you to Rev. Michelle D. Witherspoon, Rev. Jessica Harris Daum, Rev. Antoinette Moss, Rev. Pat Morrison, and Rev. Austin Carty (almost half of our Resonance Posse!) for your thorough and careful reading and insightful feedback. You each brought Rosa, Taylor, your own selves, and your faith communities to your reading of the manuscript, and I loved journeying with your comments and wisdom. This book would not be what it is without you.

Thank you to Andy for your vigilant heresy hunting and secular age-smoothness spotting, and for always bringing me back to the cross and the act of God.

Finally, thank you to Maisy, Owen, and Andy for humoring me not only as a homiletical creature (as Lisa Larges once called me) but a liturgical one. I am so blessed to receive this life together with you. How will God surprise us today?